inspire

2

PAMELA HARTMANN

NANCY DOUGLAS

ANDREW BOON

Australia • Brazil • Japan • Korea • Mexico • Singapore • Spain • United Kingdom • United States

Inspire 2
Pamela Hartmann, Nancy Douglas, and Andrew Boon

Publisher: Andrew Robinson

Executive Editor: Sean Bermingham

Senior Development Editor: Derek Mackrell

Development Editor: Claire Tan

Director of Global Marketing: Ian Martin

Product Marketing Manager: Lindsey Miller

Senior Content Project Manager: Tan Jin Hock

Manufacturing Planner: Mary Beth Hennebury

Compositor: Page 2, LLC.

Cover/Text Design: Creative Director:
Christopher Roy, Art Director: Scott Baker,
Designer: Alex Dull

Cover Photos: (front) Paul Nicklen/National
Geographic Creative, (back) Beverly Joubert/
National Geographic Creative

ISBN-13: 978-1-133-96368-4

ISBN-10: 1-133-96368-4

National Geographic Learning
20 Channel Center Street
Boston, MA 02210
USA

Cengage Learning is a leading provider of customized learning solutions with office locations around the globe, including Singapore, the United Kingdom, Australia, Mexico, Brazil, and Japan. Locate your local office at:
international.cengage.com/region

Cengage Learning products are represented in Canada by Nelson Education, Ltd.

Visit National Geographic Learning online at **NGL.Cengage.com**

Visit our corporate website at **www.cengage.com**

Printed in the United States
1 2 3 4 5 6 7 — 17 16 15 14 13

Contents

	Scope and Sequence	4
	Unit Walkthrough	6
	Acknowledgments	10
1	Food	11
2	Festivals	19
	The Big Picture 1	27
3	Cities	31
4	Jobs	39
	The Big Picture 2	47
5	Music	51
6	Journeys	59
	The Big Picture 3	67
7	Family	71
8	Nature	79
	The Big Picture 4	87
9	Happiness	91
10	Conservation	99
	The Big Picture 5	107
	Unit Notes	111
	Credits	128

Scope and Sequence

Unit	Topic	Lesson A: Listening	Conversation Focus
1	**Food**	Street Food	Talking About Food / What's your favorite street food?
2	**Festivals**	Messy Festivals	Talking About Festivals / Which festival do you like?
Review 1	The Big Picture 1		
3	**Cities**	Istanbul Walking Tour	Talking About Your City / What is an interesting area of your city?
4	**Jobs**	Barrington Irving	Talking About Jobs / What job would you like to do?
Review 2	The Big Picture 2		
5	**Music**	Music From Around the World	Talking About Music / What kind of music do you like?
6	**Journeys**	Couch Surfing or Hostels?	Talking About Travel / Have you ever been anywhere interesting?
Review 3	The Big Picture 3		
7	**Family**	A Famous Family	Talking About Families / How many people are there in your family?
8	**Nature**	My Adventure Bucket List	Talking about Adventure Travel / What's on your adventure bucket list?
Review 4	The Big Picture 4		
9	**Happiness**	What Makes You Happy?	Talking About Happiness / What do you think people need to be happy?
10	**Conservation**	Why Are They Endangered?	Talking About Endangered Species / Did you know that grizzly bears are endangered?
Review 5	The Big Picture 5		

Lesson B: Reading	Discussion Focus	Video	Expansion Activity
The Problem with Sugar	Saying you agree or disagree	Slow Food	Plan a Restaurant
Festival in the Desert	Making and responding to suggestions	The Festival of Lights	Organize a Festival
Bogotá: Buses, Bicycles, and People	Talking about problems	Urban Earth	Finding City Solutions
Future Occupations	Making predictions about the future	A Day in the Life of a Wildlife Photographer	Interview Someone About Their Job
Music with a Message / Feliciano dos Santos	Giving reasons using *because*	The Zawoses of Tanzania	Write a Song!
Bus to Antarctica / Andrew Evans	Talking about your dream holiday	The Snowman Trek	Plan an Expedition
Brazil's Changing Families	Showing you are interested	Raising Otter Babies	Family Debate
Back to Nature / Juan Martinez	Talking about pros and cons	American Frontier Journey	Make a Public Service Announcement
The Happiest Places on Earth / San Luis Obispo, U.S.A.	Comparing and contrasting two things	An Island Paradise	How to Be Happy
Solving Problems, Saving Animals	Talking about problems and solutions	Saving Orphan Elephants	Give a Persuasive Presentation

Unit Walkthrough

Unit Opener

Warm Up discussion questions introduce the unit topic.

Lesson A

Listening sections gradually progress from closed listening tasks to open discussion, providing the scaffolding students need.

Conversation sections provide both guided and personalized conversation practice.

Audio icons indicate CD and audio track numbers.

Listening activities practice a range of listening skills.

Language models in speech bubbles provide examples.

Lesson B

Reading comprehension questions check students' understanding of the reading passage.

A second **listening section** provides additional listening practice and further develops the ideas introduced in the reading passage.

Discussion sections introduce and practice functional language and expressions.

Reading passages are adapted and graded from authentic sources. They provide content input to act as a stimulus for discussion later in this section.

Split activities indicate in red where one student turns to the end of the book.

Video

Video activities give extra comprehension and vocabulary practice, and provide opportunities for authentic input, acting as a springboard for discussion.

Expansion Activity

Expansion activities encourage students to use the language they've encountered in the unit and extend themselves in freer practice.

Tip boxes provide suggestions for ways students can use technology, such as cell phones to assist them.

Unit Notes

Unit notes at the back of the book provide additional material for split activities, as well as language notes, and suggestions for additional activities.

Target vocabulary provides definitions for key topic related vocabulary from the unit.

Important language gives a summary of language structures from the unit.

Project ideas usually build upon the Expansion Activity, and provide suggestions for ways in which students can take their learning beyond the classroom.

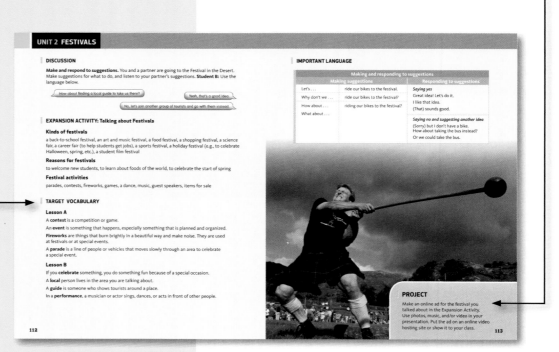

The Big Picture

There are five Big Picture sections, one after every two units. These sections review the previous two units and allow further opportunities for discussion.

Observation and discussion activities use the large photo to encourage communication and language practice.

Caption competition encourages students to think creatively about the image.

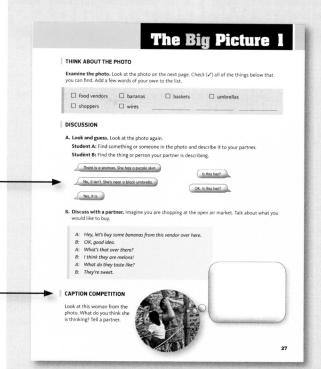

A stunning photo acts as a motivating prompt for discussion.

Review activities recycle and practice key language and vocabulary from the previous two units.

Acknowledgments

Many thanks to Andrew Robinson, William Preston, and Sean Bermingham, for their organization, guidance, and wisdom, and Andy Boon, for his invaluable input.

Pamela Hartmann

I would like to thank everyone who participated in the development of this series. Special thanks go to publisher Andrew Robinson for inviting me to be a part of this project, to Derek Mackrell for his editorial expertise and encouragement, and to Andy Boon for his invaluable support and inspiration. I am also grateful to my husband Jorge and daughter Jasmine for the love and encouragement they provided during the writing of this book.

Nancy Douglas

I would like to thank my wonderful co-authors and editorial team for their enthusiasm, ideas, and work throughout the Inspire project. I would also like to thank all the students I have ever taught—you guys ARE the inspiration!

Andrew Boon

The Authors and Publishers would like to thank the following teaching professionals for their valuable feedback during the development of this series.

Jennifer Alicea, UPR Ponce, Puerto Rico, United States; **Grace Bishop**, Houston Community College, Houston, United States; **Leonardo Escobar**, Universidad Manuela Beltra, Bogotá, Colombia; **David Fairweather**, Asahikawa Medical University, Hokkaido, Japan; **Wendy M. Gough**, St. Mary College/Nunoike Gaigo Senmon Gakko, Nagoya, Japan; **Erica Harris**, Lewis & Clark College, Portland, United States; **Ikuko Kashiwabara**, Osaka Electro-Communication University, Neyagawa, Japan; **Maureen Kelbert**, Vancouver Community College, Vancouver, Canada; **Jungryul Kim**, Korea National University of Education, Cheongwon, South Korea; **Bridget McDonald**, ELC Boston, Boston, United States; **Jill McDonough**, South Seattle Community College, Seattle, United States; **Kent McLeod**, UT Arlington English Language Institute, Mansfield, United States; **Donna Moore**, Hawaii Community College, Hilo, United States; **Nancy Nystrom**, University of Texas at San Antonio, San Antonio, United States; **Jane O'Connor**, Emory College of Arts and Sciences, Decatur, United States; **Elizabeth Ortiz**, COPEI-COPOL English Institute, Guayaquil, Ecuador; **Maeran Park**, Bukyoung National University, Busan, South Korea; **Terri Rapoport**, ELS Educational Services, Inc., Princeton, United States; **Amy Renehan**, University of Washington, Seattle, United States; **Greg Rouault**, Konan University, Hirao School of Management, Nishinomiya, Japan; **Elena Sapp**, INTO Oregon State University, Corvallis, United States; **Anne-Marie Schlender**, Austin Community College, Austin, United States; **Karen Shock**, Savannah College of Art and Design, Atlanta, United States; **Julie Thornton**, CSULB American Language Institute, Santa Ana, United States; **Rosa E. Vasquez Fernandez**, John F. Kennedy Institute of Languages, Inc., STI, Dominican Republic; **Matthew Walters**, Hongik University, Seoul, South Korea; **Christie Ward**, Central Connecticut State University, New Britain, United States; **Matthew Watterson**, Hongik University, Mapo-Gu, South Korea; **Chris Willson**, Meio University, Okinawa, Japan; **Kyungsook Yeum**, Sookmyoung Women's University, Seoul, South Korea

Food

A plate of macarons from a restaurant in New York, U.S.A.

WARM UP

Answer these questions with a partner.

1. Would you like to eat the food in the photo?
2. What is your favorite food?
3. Which country's food do you like most?

LISTENING

A. Label the map. Where do you think the food on the next page comes from? Match the food (**1** to **4**) to the places.

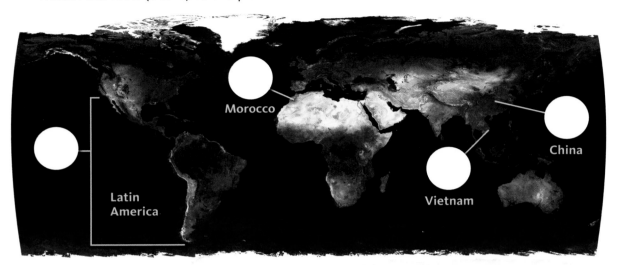

 B. Listen and check. Were your answers correct?
Track 1-01

 C. Listen for details. How does each food taste? Guess. Then circle the words you hear.
Track 1-01

1. The banh mi sandwiches taste **spicy / sweet**.
2. The grasshoppers taste **crunchy and salty / sweet and spicy**.
3. The tea is really **salty / refreshing**.
4. The ceviche tastes **delicious / gross**.

D. Talk with a partner. Which one would you like to try?

I'd like to try ceviche.

CONVERSATION

 A. Listen to the conversation.
Track 1-02

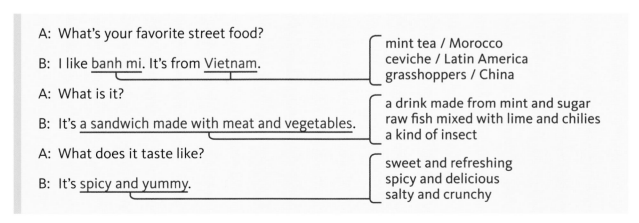

A: What's your favorite street food?

B: I like banh mi. It's from Vietnam.

A: What is it?

B: It's a sandwich made with meat and vegetables.

A: What does it taste like?

B: It's spicy and yummy.

mint tea / Morocco
ceviche / Latin America
grasshoppers / China

a drink made from mint and sugar
raw fish mixed with lime and chilies
a kind of insect

sweet and refreshing
spicy and delicious
salty and crunchy

B. Practice with a partner. Use the words on the right.

C. Practice again. Talk about foods you like.

Plurals
It's → They're
What is it? → What are they?
What does it . . . ? → What do they . . . ?

Street Food

meat

vegetables

1 banh mi sandwiches

2 grasshoppers

3 mint tea

mint

4 ceviche

lime

raw fish

13

READING

A. Read the chart. Which two countries are missing? Guess.

Track 1-03

B. Read the article. Why is a lot of sugar bad for you? Underline the reasons as you read.

The Problem with Sugar

Consumption* of Sodas
cans per person per year

1. _____	529
2. _____	501
Malta	425
Czech Republic	413
Chile	391
Norway	381
Australia	377
Iceland	333
Canada	311
Belgium	300

* Includes regular and low-calorie sodas

Worldwide, children and adults today are eating and drinking more sugar than ever before. One of the main ways people consume sugar is by drinking soda. Some cans of soda contain more than ten cubes of sugar. As the chart shows, many people have one or two cans of soda every day.

Drinking soda is only one way that people consume sugar. Too much sugar is bad for your teeth and can cause other health problems. A recent study shows that eating too much sugar can also be bad for your memory.

The mayor of New York City, Michael Bloomberg, wants to make people drink less soda. He wants to introduce a new law. It says that stores and restaurants in the city can't sell sodas in a cup larger than 16 ounces (about 0.5 liters). Some people like this law. They think it will make people drink less soda. However, some people disagree. They think people should be able to eat and drink whatever they want.

C. Reading comprehension. Are the statements below true or false?

	True	False
1. Today, people are consuming less sugar than they used to.	_____	_____
2. Too much sugar can be bad for your memory.	_____	_____
3. A new law in New York City says that only sugar-free soda can be sold.	_____	_____

D. Think about it. Here are some other food laws. Some are real and some are fake. Which ones do you think are real? Write **real** or **fake**.

Country	Law	Real?
Canada	Stores can't sell alcohol to a pregnant woman.	
Chile	Fast food restaurants can't sell "kids' meals" with a toy inside.	
Malaysia	Stores can only sell organic vegetables.	
Wales	Vending machines in hospitals can't sell sugary snacks and drinks.	

LISTENING

Track 1-04

A. Listen for the main idea. Steve and Gina are at school. What are they talking about?

   a. the price of soda   b. a new teacher   c. new food in the cafeteria

Track 1-05

B. Listen for details. Listen to the rest of the conversation. Choose the correct answer.

1. Which sentence about Gina and Steve's school is correct?

   a. You can buy only healthy soda.

   b. All sodas at the school cost more now.

   c. The school has stopped selling soda completely.

2. Why is the school doing this?

   a. The school wants students to save money.

   b. The school wants to make more money.

   c. The school wants students to drink less soda.

3. What does Gina say about France?

   a. There is a tax on soda there.

   b. Soda is healthier there.

   c. Schools can't sell soda there.

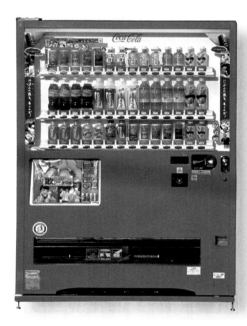

DISCUSSION

Saying you agree or disagree. What do you think of the laws at the top of the page? Use the language below to give your opinion.

> I think this is a good idea.

> I agree. I think it will make people eat more healthily.

> I disagree. In my opinion, people should eat and drink anything they want.

Slow Food

A traditional food store in Tuscany, Italy

BEFORE YOU WATCH

About the video. Greve is a small city in Italy. It's in an area that is famous for its local food. The mayors of Greve and three other Italian cities started a group called the Slow Cities League. They are part of the Slow Food movement, which has thousands of members worldwide.

Talk with a partner. Look at the pictures. Discuss these questions.

1. What food can you see in the pictures?
2. What is fast food? Do you eat fast food?
3. The video is called *Slow Food*. What do you think slow food is?

WHILE YOU WATCH

Watch and check. Check (✓) the expressions that describe life in Greve and the Slow Food movement.

☐ local ingredients
☐ making food the traditional way
☐ moving into the fast lane
☐ finding the same food everywhere
☐ taking your time
☐ respecting the specialness of every food

AFTER YOU WATCH

A. What do you remember? Are the statements below true or false?

	True	False
1. The Slow Food movement started in America.	_____	_____
2. The goals of the Slow Food movement are about more than food.	_____	_____
3. The Slow Food movement has 100,000 members.	_____	_____
4. People in Greve still make cheese by hand these days.	_____	_____

B. Work with a partner. Choose three special kinds of food from your city or country. Complete the chart.

	Food	What is it?
1.	takoyaki (from Japan)	balls made from octopus
2.		
3.		
4.		

C. Join another pair. Compare your charts.
Explain why the foods you chose are special.

> I think takoyaki is special. It's a delicious snack made from octopus and flour, with sauce on it. It's a great snack.

Traditional fruit sweets at a
Slow Food festival in Turin, Italy

17

Plan a Restaurant

You are starting a new restaurant, but you need people to give you money to start it.

A. Plan your restaurant. Work with a partner. Answer these questions. **See page 111 for examples,** or use ideas of your own.

1. Where is the restaurant?
2. What kind of food do you sell? Give some examples.
3. What is interesting or special about your restaurant?

B. Make a poster. With your partner, make a poster to show your restaurant ideas.

C. Present your restaurant to another pair, using your poster. Then listen and take notes on their restaurant. Ask questions. Then find another pair to talk to.

D. Review your notes with your partner. Imagine you are giving money to a new restaurant. In your opinion, which restaurant is the best? Why?

E. Tell the class your answer. The restaurant with the most votes wins.

Do an online search for "types of restaurants" to learn about different places to eat. Use this information to help you create your own restaurant.

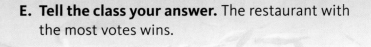

Ithaa Undersea Restaurant at the Conrad Hotel, Maldives, is five meters under the sea.

Festivals

Masked dancers at the
Black-necked Crane Festival
in Bhutan

WARM UP

Answer these questions with
a partner.

1. What can you see in the picture?
2. Which festivals are popular in
   your country?
3. Which festivals have you been to?

Messy

mud

The Mud Festival

LISTENING

Track 1-06 **A. Listen and circle the answers.**

The Mud Festival is held in **South Korea** / **Japan** in **June** / **July**. Tomatina, the tomato festival, is held every **August** / **October** in **Spain** / **Mexico**. Both festivals are held in **spring** / **summer**.

Track 1-07 **B. Listen for details.** Listen to the rest of the interview. Which festival(s) do the sentences below describe?

	The Mud Festival	Tomatina
1. It takes place near a beach.	_____	_____
2. People go there from all over the world.	_____	_____
3. There are fireworks.	_____	_____
4. There is a cooking contest.	_____	_____
5. There is a parade.	_____	_____
6. You can go swimming.	_____	_____

C. Discuss with a partner. Which festival would you like to go to? Why?

I'd like to go to Tomatina. It looks really fun.

Yeah! But it looks really messy!

Festivals

CONVERSATION

Track 1-08

A. Listen to the conversation.

A: Which festival do you like?

B: I like <u>Tomatina</u>. It's a festival in <u>Spain</u>.

| the Mud Festival / Korea |
| the Snow Festival / Japan |
| Mardi Gras / Brazil |

A: Really? When is it?

B: It's a <u>summer</u> festival. It's held in <u>August</u>.

| summer / July |
| winter / February |
| winter / February or March |

A: Yeah? What happens there?

B: <u>People throw tomatoes at each other</u>.

| People play with mud |
| You can see many things made from snow |
| You can listen to music and watch a parade |

B. Practice with a partner. Use the words on the right.

C. Practice again. Talk about festivals you know.

tomatoes

Tomatina

READING

A. Prediction. You are going to read about a festival in the Sahara desert. Which of these do you think you can do at the festival?

☐ watch music performances   ☐ stay in a hotel   ☐ see a camel race

B. Read the poster on page 23. Check your ideas in **A**. Then complete the table.

Track 1-09

When is it?	What can you do there?	What should you bring?	How do you get there?
January or February			
Where is it?			
the Sahara desert			

C. Which festival is most interesting? Rank the three festivals below from **1** to **3**. Share your list with a partner.

_____ the Festival in the Desert   _____ the Mud Festival   _____ Tomatina

LISTENING

A. Listen for details. Listen to three cell phone messages. Then listen to the three responses. Circle the correct information in each sentence.

Track 1-10

1. Maria calls Aya because she wants to **go to a festival / do a project on a festival**.

2. Manny calls Erik because he wants to **drive / take the bus** to the North Beach Festival.

3. Lisa calls Kira because she wants to **meet at / leave for** the Outside Lands Music Festival at 12:30.

B. Listen for gist. Now listen to the three responses. Do the speakers say yes or no to each suggestion?

Track 1-11

1. **yes / no**   2. **yes / no**   3. **yes / no**

DISCUSSION

Making and responding to suggestions. You and a partner are going to the Festival in the Desert. Make suggestions for what to do, and listen to your partner's suggestions.
Student A: Use the language below. **Student B: Turn to page 112.**

Let's buy a tent to take with us.

I like that idea. Let's do it.

No, why don't we sleep in the car instead?

FESTIVAL IN THE DESERT

Timbuktu, Mali

GENERAL INFORMATION

For three days every January or February, people of the Sahara desert come together for this festival of traditional culture. They meet and celebrate with song, dance, poetry, and other cultural traditions.

DON'T MISS

During the day
- the camel races (The fastest and most beautiful win.)
- sword fighting and other contests
- the arts shows and presentations by local people

At night
- performances by local and global musicians

WHAT TO BRING There are no hotels, so you'll need a sleeping bag, tent, food, and water. It is very hot in the daytime so bring lightweight clothes. However, it can be cold at night, so bring a sweater or warm jacket for the evening.

GETTING THERE

You'll need a truck or camel to get to the festival. It's about two hours from the town of Timbuktu, Mali. It is also a good idea to use a local guide. This person can drive to the festival and help you during your stay.

temple

lights

fireworks

The Festival of Lights

Diwali celebrations in Leicester, England, are the biggest outside India.

BEFORE YOU WATCH

About the video. The video shows a traditional Indian celebration. Diwali, known as the "festival of lights," is a five-day festival that falls sometime between mid-October and mid-November. It is one of the most important festivals of the year in India, and is also held in other Indian communities around the world.

Make predictions. Look at the pictures. What do you think people do during Diwali?

_____ visit a temple	_____ light candles
_____ buy flowers	_____ draw pictures with sand
_____ watch fireworks	_____ see a parade
_____ join a cooking contest	_____ go to the beach
_____ buy new clothes	_____ look at beautiful lights

WHILE YOU WATCH

Check your answers. As you watch, check your answers to the question above.

AFTER YOU WATCH

A. What do you remember? Are the statements below true or false?

		True	False
1.	Afternoon is the best time to visit the flower market.	____	____
2.	Rangoli are usually pictures of flowers.	____	____
3.	People share food with their neighbors.	____	____
4.	Shops are closed during Diwali.	____	____

B. Think of a festival you know. Complete the table below.

Name of festival	When is it?	What happens?

C. Talk with a partner. Tell a partner about your festival.

candles

sand

A family in India celebrating Diwali

Organize a Festival

You are going to make an advertisement to tell people about a festival.

A. Plan a festival. Work with a partner to complete the table. **See page 112 for ideas.**

What kind of festival?	Where and when?	What can people do?
e.g., a music festival	e.g., the beach	e.g., listen to bands

B. Create an advertisement to tell people about your festival.

C. Present your festival to another pair. Then listen and take notes on theirs. Ask questions. Switch pairs. Learn about all the festivals in your class.

Find photos online or take photos around school to use in your advertisement.

D. Choose one festival you like the most. Suggest going to it to your partner.

A man wearing a kilt throws a hammer at the Glenfinnan Highland Games, Scotland.

THINK ABOUT THE PHOTO

Examine the photo. Look at the photo on the next page. Check (✔) all of the things below that you can find. Add a few words of your own to the list.

☐ food vendors ☐ bananas ☐ baskets ☐ umbrellas

☐ shoppers ☐ wires _____ _____ _____

DISCUSSION

A. Look and guess. Look at the photo again.

Student A: Find something or someone in the photo and describe it to your partner.

Student B: Find the thing or person your partner is describing.

There is a woman. She has a purple skirt.

Is this her?

No, it isn't. She's near a black umbrella.

OK. Is this her?

Yes, it is.

B. Discuss with a partner. Imagine you are shopping at the open air market. Talk about what you would like to buy.

> A: *Hey, let's buy some bananas from this vendor over here.*
> B: *OK, good idea.*
> A: *What's that over there?*
> B: *I think they are melons!*
> A: *What do they taste like?*
> B: *They're sweet.*

CAPTION COMPETITION

Look at this woman from the photo. What do you think she is thinking? Tell a partner.

An open air market in Indonesia sells vegetables and items for the home.

Review 1

A. Complete the sentences. Match each half to complete the sentences.

1. This Indian curry ● ● a. use a local guide.
2. A vending machine ● ● b. is held in February.
3. People at the mud festival ● ● c. is tasty but very spicy.
4. Sapporo snow festival ● ● d. get really messy.
5. At the Festival in the Desert, ● ● e. sells snacks and drinks.
   it's a good idea to

B. Do you agree or disagree with these statements? Discuss your answers with a partner.

	Agree	Disagree
Tea is a really refreshing drink.	_____	_____
People should drink less soda.	_____	_____
Fast food is more delicious than slow food.	_____	_____
The Korean mud festival looks fun.	_____	_____
The Festival in the Desert is interesting.	_____	_____

C. Complete these statements with your own ideas. Then share your ideas with a partner.

1. _____ is / are salty.
2. _____ is / are gross.
3. _____ is / are spicy.
4. _____ takes place in the fall.
5. _____ is held in July.

D. Practice the conversation. Complete the conversation with the missing words. Then practice with a partner. Then have a conversation about a food you know.

let's	taste	from	street	meat

John: Hey! What's your favorite _____ food?

Sue: Well, I love souvlaki. It's _____ Greece.

John: What is it?

Sue: It's small pieces of _____ and vegetables served on bread.

John: What does it _____ like?

Sue: It's delicious. In fact, you can buy one from that vendor over there.

John: _____ get one.

Cities

Hong Kong from above

3

WARM UP

Answer these questions with a partner.

1. Do you think it's better to live in a city or in the country? Why?

2. Which is your favorite city?

3. Which city do you most want to visit?

31

ISTANBUL
Walking Tour

near Taksim Square

the Spice Bazaar

Whirling Dervishes

LISTENING

Track 1-12

A. Quiz. What do you know about Istanbul? Read and circle the correct answers. Then listen to the beginning of a walking tour of Istanbul and check.

> Istanbul is a city in (**Turkey** / **Greece**), and is in both Europe and (**Asia** / **Africa**). It has been a city for (**only 400** / **more than 2,000**) years, and is (**quite small** / **one of the largest cities in the world**).

Track 1-13

B. Listen for gist. Now listen to the rest of the walking tour. Number the photos **1** to **4** in the order the tour group visits them.

Track 1-14

C. Listen for details. Listen and circle the words you hear.

1. This area is **lively** / **quiet**, with lots of **trendy** / **expensive** stores.
2. This is an **ancient** / **modern** tradition. They move **while music plays** / **in silence**.
3. This area has many popular **hotels** / **restaurants and cafés**.
4. This place started in **1363** / **1663**. It is usually **empty** / **crowded** by the afternoon.

D. Discuss with a partner. Which of the four places on the tour would you most like to see?

> I'd like to see Galata Bridge. It sounds really interesting.

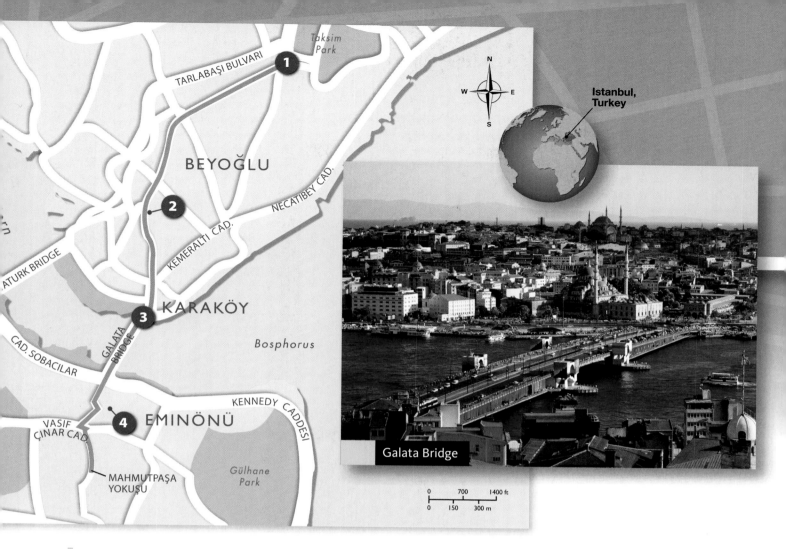

Istanbul, Turkey

Galata Bridge

CONVERSATION

Track 1-15

A. Listen to the conversation.

A: What's an interesting area of your city?

B: I really like <u>Harajuku</u>.

> Little India
> Knightsbridge
> Chinatown

A: Why do you like it?

B: Because there are a lot of <u>great clothing stores</u> there.

> Indian restaurants
> trendy stores
> interesting stalls

A: What can you do there?

B: You can <u>buy really cool clothes</u>.

> eat great Indian food
> go window shopping
> buy unusual things

B. Practice with a partner. Use the words on the right.

C. Talk with a partner. Use the language above to talk about cities you know.

> The Hongdae district in Seoul has lots of trendy clubs and stores. One of my favorite places is . . .

READING

Track 1-16

A. Reading passage. Read about Bogotá, Colombia. As you read, underline the problems the city had. Circle the solutions to those problems.

Fixing the city

Bogotá:
Buses, Bicycles, and People

Bogota, Colombia

Downtown Bogotá

Bogotá, Colombia, is a city of seven million people. Fifteen years ago, there wasn't enough public transportation. There was too much traffic, and air pollution was a problem. Then in 1998, the city made some big changes.

First, it increased the tax on gas and used the money to create a new bus system. Today, almost 500,000 people use these buses every day. To reduce traffic, Bogotá also put more bike lanes around the city. Now, almost 350,000 people commute to school or work on their bicycles. On Sundays and holidays, the city's main streets are also closed to cars. Two million people visit Bogotá's car-free streets every Sunday to walk, bike, shop, and relax.

B. Scanning for numbers. What do the numbers below refer to? Match them.

1. 350,000   a. people who use the bus every day
2. 500,000   b. people who use the car-free streets every Sunday
3. 2 million   c. people who commute by bicycle

C. Discuss with a partner. Which form of transportation do you use most often: a car, public transportation, or a bicycle? Does your city have a car-free area? If so, where? Is it popular?

LISTENING

A. Listen for details. Which cities are being talked about? Number them **1** to **3**.

Track 1-17

City		Problem			Solution
_____ London	•	• too much traffic	•	•	electric buses
_____ Singapore	•	• too much air pollution	•	•	a new park
_____ Mexico City	•	• not enough green space in the city	•	•	a fee to enter the area

B. Listen for the main idea. Match each city to its problem and a solution.

Track 1-18

DISCUSSION

Talking about problems. What are some problems in your city or neighborhood? Talk about them with a partner. Use the language below.

> There are too many cars, and there's too much street noise.

> Yeah. And there aren't enough parks, and there isn't enough green space.

These 50-meter tall "super trees" in Singapore help to collect rain water, clean the air, and keep the city cool.

35

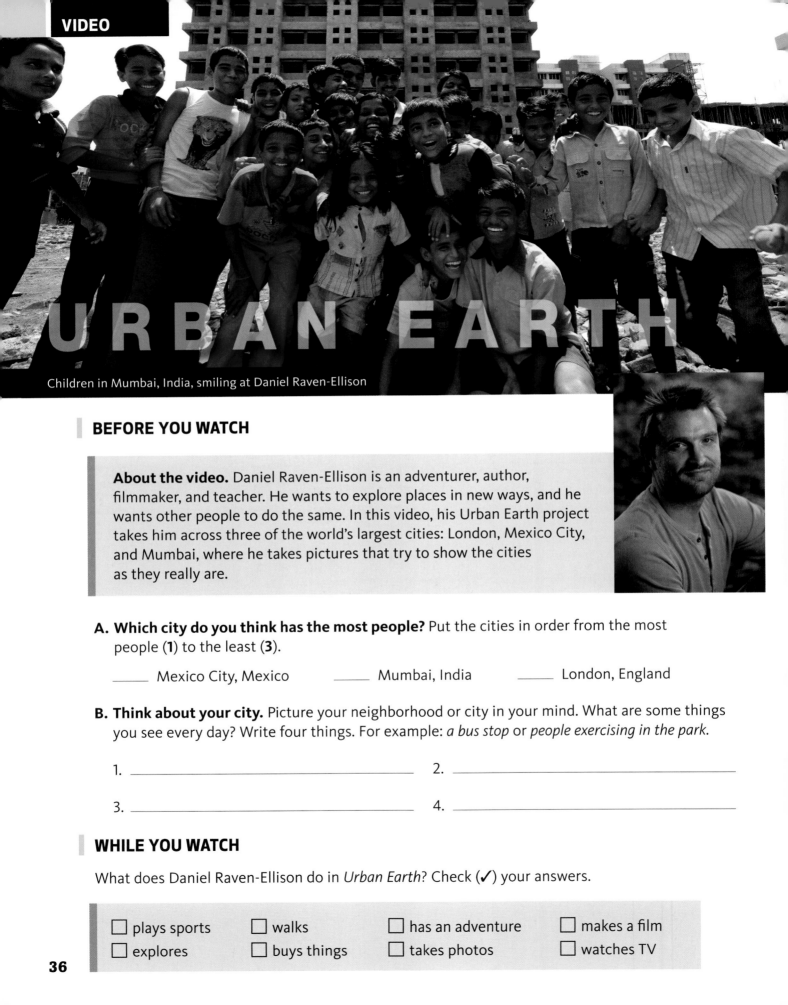

URBAN EARTH

Children in Mumbai, India, smiling at Daniel Raven-Ellison

BEFORE YOU WATCH

About the video. Daniel Raven-Ellison is an adventurer, author, filmmaker, and teacher. He wants to explore places in new ways, and he wants other people to do the same. In this video, his Urban Earth project takes him across three of the world's largest cities: London, Mexico City, and Mumbai, where he takes pictures that try to show the cities as they really are.

A. Which city do you think has the most people? Put the cities in order from the most people (**1**) to the least (**3**).

_____ Mexico City, Mexico   _____ Mumbai, India   _____ London, England

B. Think about your city. Picture your neighborhood or city in your mind. What are some things you see every day? Write four things. For example: *a bus stop* or *people exercising in the park*.

1. _____   2. _____

3. _____   4. _____

WHILE YOU WATCH

What does Daniel Raven-Ellison do in *Urban Earth*? Check (✓) your answers.

☐ plays sports	☐ walks	☐ has an adventure	☐ makes a film
☐ explores	☐ buys things	☐ takes photos	☐ watches TV

AFTER YOU WATCH

A. What do you remember? Are the statements below true or false?

	True	False
1. Daniel films his movies while driving across the cities.	_____	_____
2. Daniel thinks the bigger cities grow, the more we know about them.	_____	_____
3. Daniel wants people to help each other make their cities better.	_____	_____
4. Daniel thinks that watching TV can be an adventure.	_____	_____
5. Daniel wants other people to go on adventures.	_____	_____

B. Discuss these questions in small groups.

1. Look at your list from **Before You Watch B**. Did you see the same things in the video? What was different?

2. Which areas in your city do you think you know very well? Are there some areas you don't usually go to? Why?

3. Which place in your city do you escape to? How is it different from other areas in the city? What can you do there?

> I escape to the old city walls in Seoul. Other areas in Seoul are crowded, and there is traffic. But there, it's quiet. I can walk or sit and read.

Mexico City, Mexico

Finding city solutions

The mayor has asked for suggestions for how to improve your city. Work with a group.

A. Identify the problems. Think of things or places in your city that have problems. Make a list.

Problems

B. Think of solutions. As a group, make a list of suggestions to fix the problems you identified.

Solutions

C. Prepare your presentation. Make a presentation to show other people your problems and solutions.

D. Give your presentation. Show your presentation to other people. Watch their presentations. Who has the best suggestions?

Find photos online and use presentation software to support your presentation.

This stream in Seoul used to be covered in cement, and there was a highway on top. In 2005 the highway was removed, and the stream was made into the popular Cheonggyecheon recreation area.

Jobs

A tree scientist studying a eucalyptus tree in Australia

4

WARM UP

Answer these questions with a partner.

1. Do you know anyone who has an interesting job?

2. If you could have any job, what would you like to do?

3. What jobs do you think will be popular ten years from now?

BARRINGTON IRVING

Barrington Irving flies a plane hand-built by students at Experience Aviation.

LISTENING

Track 1-19

A. Listen for job titles. What jobs has Barrington Irving done? Listen and circle.

Jobs ending in *–er/–or*	Jobs ending in *–ist*	Other
actor	artist	coach
airplane cleaner	dentist	entrepreneur
explorer	journalist	pilot
teacher	scientist	shop assistant

Track 1-19

B. Listen for details. Listen again and circle the correct answers.

1. Barrington Irving played (**football / tennis / hockey**) in high school.
2. Irving's plane is called the (*Experience / Inspiration / Memorial*).
3. Irving became the youngest person to fly solo around the world at the age of (**15 / 23 / 28**).
4. Irving's company helps students learn about (**math and science / starting a company / making money**).

C. Discuss with a partner. Which of Barrington Irving's jobs would you most like to do?

> I'd like to be an explorer. I think it would be really exciting.

CONVERSATION

Track **1-20**

A. Listen to the conversation.

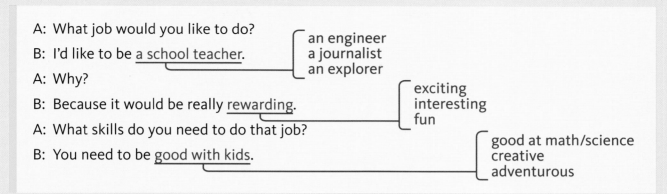

A: What job would you like to do?

B: I'd like to be a school teacher.
 — an engineer
 — a journalist
 — an explorer

A: Why?

B: Because it would be really rewarding.
 — exciting
 — interesting
 — fun

A: What skills do you need to do that job?

B: You need to be good with kids.
 — good at math/science
 — creative
 — adventurous

B. Practice with a partner. Use the words on the right.

C. Practice again. Talk about jobs you would like to do.

Barrington Irving arriving home after his first solo trip around the world

READING

A. **Prediction.** The reading passage describes two jobs: space tour guide and bioengineer. Which of these jobs do you think exists now?

Track 1-21

B. **Split reading. Student A:** Read the passage below about space tour guides.
Student B: Read about bioengineers on page 116.

FUTURE OCCUPATIONS
SPACE TOUR GUIDE

What occupations will be popular in the future? A recent study lists over 100 possibilities. Here's one: space tour guide.

In the future, experts say that humans will have stations on the moon and possibly Mars. A new kind of tourism—space travel—is just beginning. Today, there are companies, such as Virgin Galactic, that are already taking reservations for future commercial flights into space.

In time, says the study, space travel companies will need tour guides to take visitors on trips to the moon and beyond. Guides will need experience working with the public. They will also need to know about the planets and other objects in space. If you have these skills and an interest in space travel, being a cosmic tour guide could be the perfect job for you. Just plan to be away from home for long periods of time.

Mark Shuttleworth (bottom) was the world's second space tourist. In 2002, he paid 20 million US dollars to spend seven days on the International Space Station.

C. **Work with a partner.** Which job(s) are these statements about? **Student A:** Ask your partner questions to help you complete the table below. **Student B:** Turn to page 116.

	space tour guide	bioengineer
1. This job will allow you to help athletes.	_____	_____
2. This job will take you away from home for a long time.	_____	_____
3. This job will help people live healthily for longer.	_____	_____
4. This job will be more popular in the future.	_____	_____
5. To do this job, you need to know about science.	_____	_____

> Will bioengineers help people live healthily for longer?

> Yes, they will.

D. Discuss with a partner. Would you like to be a space tour guide or bioengineer? Why or why not?

> I'd really like to be a space tour guide. I think it would be amazing.

> Oh, not me. I think it would be scary.

LISTENING

Track 1-23

A. Listen for opinions. What does the man say about each job? Circle the correct opinions.

Job	Opinion	Reasons
1. space tour guide	He **likes / doesn't like** it.	a. You'll have to work **long hours / far away**. b. It will **pay well / be hard on the body**.
2. bioengineer	He **likes / doesn't like** it.	a. People will live **longer and healthier lives / have more free time**. b. It will help people improve their **minds / bodies**.

Track 1-23

B. Listen for details. The man gives reasons for his opinions. Circle the answers.

DISCUSSION

Making predictions about the future. With a partner, make a list of six jobs. Then answer these questions for each. Use the language below.

Ten years from now . . .

1. will this job exist? Why or why not?
2. will a computer or robot do the job instead of humans? Why or why not?
3. will more women or men do this job? Why?

> In ten years, fashion designers will probably still exist because people will still want beautiful clothes.

> People definitely won't work in video rental stores, because everyone will watch movies online.

A Day in the Life of a Wildlife Photographer

Botswana

Beverly Joubert photographing meerkats in Botswana

BEFORE YOU WATCH

About the video. Dereck and Beverly Joubert are wildlife photographers in Africa. This video shows what their job is like, and how they take their amazing photos.

Prediction. Which of these do you think you need in order to be a wildlife photographer in Africa?

☐ creativity   ☐ patience   ☐ a lot of money   ☐ hard work   ☐ bravery

WHILE YOU WATCH

A. Watch and check your answers above.

B. What animals do you see? Write the names of three animals in the video.

_____   _____   _____

AFTER YOU WATCH

A. What do you remember? Choose the correct answer.

1. How long have the Jouberts worked in Africa?

   a. about 5 years   b. about 15 years   c. about 25 years

2. To get near animals without scaring them, Dereck dresses as _____.

   a. a lion   b. a zebra   c. a cheetah

3. The Jouberts have spent as long as _____ studying a single animal.

   a. three months   b. three years   c. eight years

4. Where do the Jouberts spend most of their time?

   a. at home   b. in a tent   c. in their car

5. In total, how many films have the Jouberts made?

   a. 12   b. 22   c. 32

B. What do you think? Would you like to do the Jouberts' job? Check (✓) the sentence that describes your opinion.

☐ Yes! Definitely!   ☐ No way!   ☐ Maybe. It depends.

C. Talk with a partner. Explain your answer in **B**.

Dereck Joubert filming an African elephant mother and baby

Interview someone about their job.

You are going to research a job and interview a partner about their job.

A. Read the interview. Amber Case is a "Cyborg Anthropologist"—she studies people's relationships with technology. Match the questions in the box below with her answers. One question is extra.

1. What's the best part of the job?
2. What do you do in this job?
3. What skills do you need for this job?
4. What's the worst part of the job?

Name: Amber Case   **Job Title:** Cyborg Anthropologist

Question: _____

Amber Case: Cell phones and computers are a big part of our lives these days.
A cyborg anthropologist studies these tools and how they are changing us.

Question: _____

AC: You need to understand different types of technology. Research skills are important too.

Question: _____

AC: It combines two of my favorite things: studying people and working with technology.

B. Research a job. Choose an interesting job, and write it down. Then answer questions **1** to **4** in **A** about your job.

_____

C. Interview a partner about his or her job. Start with "What do you do in this job?" and then use the other questions in **A**. Ask extra questions to learn more. Take turns.

D. Change partners. After you've finished interviewing, tell your group about someone you interviewed and what you learned about his or her job.

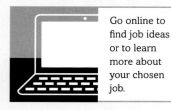

Go online to find job ideas or to learn more about your chosen job.

Amber Case

THINK ABOUT THE PHOTO

A. Prediction. Look at the photo on the next page. Photographer Joel Sartore took this photo for *National Geographic* in 1995. Where do you think he took it?

   a. a museum   b. a zoo   c. a national park   d. a store

B. Examine the photo. Look at the photo again and check (✓) all of the things below that you can find. Add a few words of your own to the list.

☐ janitor   ☐ sheep   ☐ duster   ☐ mountain   ☐ rocks

☐ crane   _____   _____   _____

DISCUSSION

A. Describe the photo. Work with a partner. Take turns describing the photo to each other.

> I see five sheep in the picture.

> The janitor is cleaning one of the sheep.

B. Look at the photo again. Imagine you can interview the janitor in the photo about his job. What questions will you ask? Make a list.

C. Interview a partner. Take turns as interviewer and janitor and interview each other.

CAPTION COMPETITION

What do you think the man in the photo is thinking? Tell a partner.

A janitor cleans sheep in Nebraska, U.S.A.

A. Match opposites. Draw lines to match the words on the left with their opposites. Then make your own sentences using these words and share them with your partner.

1. quiet ● ● ancient

2. modern ● ● uncool

3. empty ● ● worst

4. trendy ● ● lively

5. best ● ● crowded

B. Write the jobs. Then share your ideas with a partner. Does he or she agree with you?

1. I stay behind the camera and tell actors what to do. I'm a(n) _____.

2. I find and write the news for newspapers or magazines. I'm a(n) _____.

3. Like Edison, who created the light bulb, I make new things. I'm a(n) _____.

4. I work at an office. I welcome visitors and answer the phone. I'm a(n) _____.

5. I take photos of wild animals for a magazine. I'm a(n) _____.

C. Write and share sentences. Write five of your own sentences about jobs and share them with your partner.

D. Guess the city. Work with a partner. Write a list of cities that you know. Show your partner the list. Describe one city to your partner and have your partner guess.

> This city is a great place. It is very lively. There are many great shops.

> Is it in Turkey?

> Yes, it is.

> Is it Istanbul?

> Yes.

E. Make predictions about your classmates.

> In ten years, Hassan will be a famous movie director.

> Jeewon won't be living in Seoul. She will move to Paris and be a fashion designer.

5

Music

A traditional drummer performing at a Japanese music festival

WARM UP

Answer these questions with a partner.

1. How often do you listen to music? Where?
2. Can you play a musical instrument?
3. Does your country have any traditional music?

LISTENING

Track 1-24

A. Listen to music. Look at the three photos. Then listen. What instrument do you hear? Number the photos **1** to **3**.

Track 1-25

B. Listen for country names. Where is each instrument from? Match each instrument to its country.

1. steel drums • • a. Australia
2. didgeridoo • • b. Mongolia
3. horsehead violin • • c. Trinidad and Tobago

Track 1-26

C. Listen for details. Answer the questions below.

Which instrument...	steel drums	didgeridoo	horsehead violin
is good for your health?	_____	_____	_____
was invented in the 1940s?	_____	_____	_____
is made from old oil containers?	_____	_____	_____
is the national instrument of its country?	_____	_____	_____
Which two instruments...			
are played all over the world today?	_____	_____	_____
are very old?	_____	_____	_____
used to be played only by men?	_____	_____	_____

D. Discuss with a partner. Which of these three instruments do you like most?

> I really like the didgeridoo. I love its sound.

CONVERSATION

Track 1-27

A. Listen to the conversation.

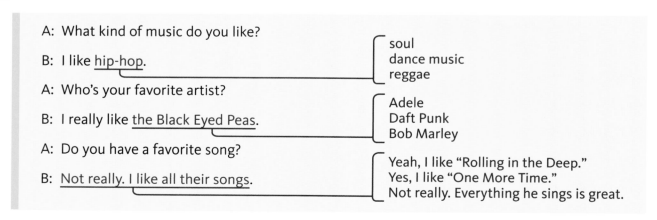

A: What kind of music do you like?

B: I like hip-hop.

A: Who's your favorite artist?

B: I really like the Black Eyed Peas.

A: Do you have a favorite song?

B: Not really. I like all their songs.

soul
dance music
reggae

Adele
Daft Punk
Bob Marley

Yeah, I like "Rolling in the Deep."
Yes, I like "One More Time."
Not really. Everything he sings is great.

B. Practice with a partner. Use the words on the right.

C. Practice again. Talk about music you know.

MUSIC FROM AROUND THE WORLD

steel drums

didgeridoo

horsehead violin

A. Prediction. "Making a difference" means doing things to help other people. How do you think Feliciano dos Santos makes a difference?

☐ by giving concerts to raise money
☐ by singing about social issues
☐ by teaching young people how to play music

Track 1-28 **B. Read.** Read the article and find the ways Feliciano dos Santos makes a difference.

Music with a Message

Feliciano dos Santos is a famous African musician. He comes from a poor village in Mozambique. As a child, he got very sick because his village didn't have clean water. This is still a problem in many places all over his country.

Today, dos Santos sings about this **social issue** and others. One of his most popular songs is "Wash Your Hands." He travels around Mozambique, visits different villages, and sings the song with people. The message in his lyrics is this: People need to wash their hands to **prevent** serious diseases. Dos Santos entertains people and teaches them. "You have to use your **talent** to do good things," he says "Everyone has a responsibility to do at least one thing to **benefit** the world."

" We wash our hands for the children to stay healthy for the uncles to stay healthy for the moms to stay healthy . . . "

— from Wash Your Han
by Feliciano dos San

C. Guess the meaning of vocabulary. Match the words from the passage with their meanings.

1. social issue   ●   ● a. something good
2. prevent   ●   ● b. a skill or ability to do something well
3. talent   ●   ● c. something people worry about
4. benefit   ●   ● d. to stop something before it happens

D. Discuss with a partner. Do you know any other musicians who are making a difference? How?

LISTENING

Track 1-29

A. Listen for the main idea. Match each musician to his message.

Jack Johnson   ●   ● stay away from drugs

Jake Shimabukuro   ●   ● protect the environment

Track 1-29

B. Listen for details. Which person do these statements match? Write **a–g** in the chart.

a. is a musician   **c.** lives in Hawaii   **e.** visits schools

b. plays the ukulele   **d.** plays the guitar   **f.** tells people to not use plastic bags

Jack Johnson

a

Jake Shimabukuro

DISCUSSION

Giving reasons using *because*. Which of the three musicians in this unit—Feliciano dos Santos, Jack Johnson, and Jake Shimabukuro—has the most important message? Tell a partner and say why you think so.

> I think Jack Johnson's work is more important because he helps people save the environment.

> That's true, but I think Feliciano dos Santos's message is most important because he helps prevent diseases.

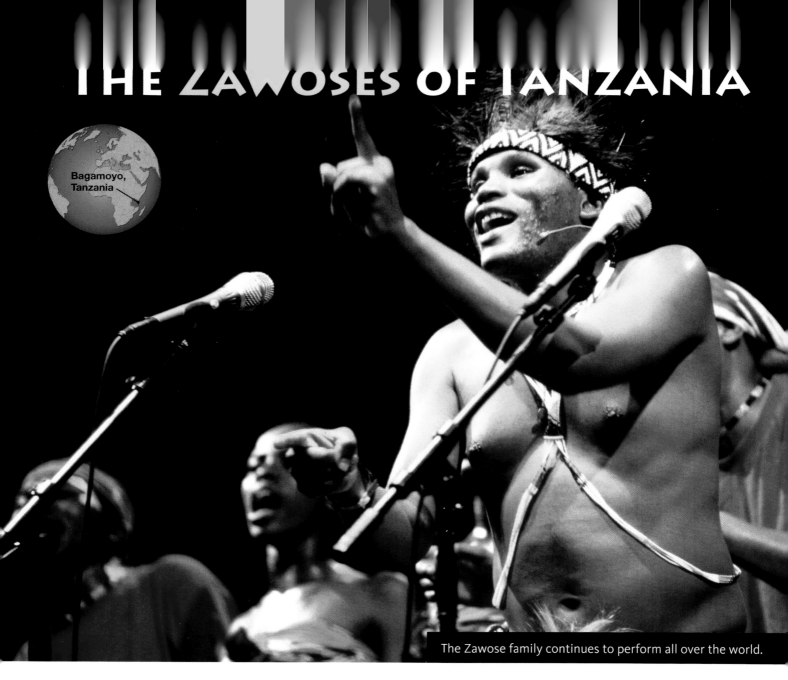

THE ZAWOSES OF TANZANIA

Bagamoyo, Tanzania

The Zawose family continues to perform all over the world.

BEFORE YOU WATCH

About the video. Dr. Hukwe Zawose is a master musician from Tanzania. He is also popular around the world. His family are not just performers sharing their music with the world, but also protectors of their musical and cultural traditions.

Vocabulary matching. You will hear the words below in the video. What do you think they mean? Match each word with its definition.

1. WOMAD ●	● a.	a traditional Tanzanian musical instrument
2. Wagogo ●	● b.	a tribe of people from Tanzania
3. Zingira ●	● c.	an international music festival

WHILE YOU WATCH

Sequencing. Number the events **1** to **4** in the order they appear in the video.

_____ Hukwe's daughter, Tabu, dances and sings.   _____ Grandfather Ubi makes an instrument.

_____ The Zawoses record an album.   _____ The music festival begins.

AFTER YOU WATCH

A. What do you remember? Complete the information about the video using the words in the box.

album	culture	his father	musician
neighbors	nephew	new	WOMAD

In Tanzania, Dr. Hukwe Zawose is a well-known local 1. _____. His musical
group is made up of his family and 2. _____. Hukwe learnt to play and make
instruments from 3. _____. With his 4. _____, Charles, he
is sharing Wagogo music with the whole world. At 5. _____, Hukwe and
Charles have a chance to meet and learn from other musicians.

The Zawoses' music is becoming more popular. So Hukwe and Charles are working with a
Canadian producer to make a(n) 6. _____. They're combining traditional
Wagogo music with 7. _____ sounds. It's important for the Zawoses to keep
their own 8. _____, and thus preserve Wagogo music for future generations.

B. Work with a partner. Complete the chart below.

1. What kind(s) of music do you like?   3. When do you listen to this kind of music?
2. Who are your favorite bands or musicians?   4. How does it make you feel?

Kind(s) of music	Favorite band/musician	When you listen	How it makes you feel

C. Discuss with a partner. Share your answers with your partner.

> I like to listen to classical music. I listen to Beethoven when I study. It helps me relax.

> I listen to hip hop. I listen to Jay-Z when I'm exercising. It gives me energy.

Write a Song!

You are going to write a song with a message about a social issue where you live.

A. Choose a social issue to write a song about. Our social issue is _____ .

B. Write a short song about the issue. Suggest ways that people can do something to solve the problem. If you can, think of music to go with your lyrics.

C. Share your song with the class. Say the name of your song and then perform it or read out the lyrics.

D. Vote. Which group had the most creative and fun song? What social issue was it about? What was its message?

Use the Internet to learn more about a social issue, or to find background music to use in your song.

Feliciano dos Santos (left) and his band

Journeys

6

The trail to Misty Fiords National Monument in Alaska, U.S.A.

WARM UP

Answer these questions with a partner.

1. Have you traveled much in your own country?
2. Have you traveled overseas?
3. Where would you like to travel to?

LISTENING

A. Read and think. Read the information below. Imagine you are going to travel somewhere. Would you rather couch surf or stay in a hostel?

Couch surfing or hostels?

CouchSurfing International is a social networking service for travelers in which hosts open their homes to travelers. Travelers stay with the hosts for free. In 2013, the site had over 5 million members in 200 countries.

A *hostel* is an inexpensive place to stay when you travel. Usually, you share a room, bathroom, and eating area with other travelers.

B. Listen for pros. Before you listen, read the sentences in the chart below. Can you guess the answers for **1** to **7**? Then listen and check answers **1** to **4**.

free	locals	cheap	noisy	meet	out	short	tourists

	pros	**cons**
Staying in a hostel	1. It's _____. 2. It's a great way to _____ people.	5. It's _____. 6. In some, you must stay _____ all day.
Couch surfing	3. One of the main benefits: It's _____. 4. You can learn things and go places most _____ don't.	7. Sometimes you can only stay for a _____ time in someone's home.

C. Listen for cons. Listen to the rest of the conversation. Check your answers for sentences **5** to **7**.

D. Discuss with a partner. What are some other pros and cons of both kinds of accommodation?

> One good thing about staying in a hostel is that you can meet lots of people.

> That's true, but you only meet other tourists, not locals.

CONVERSATION

A. Listen to the conversation.

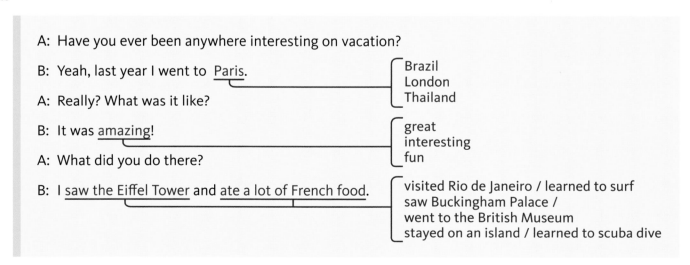

A: Have you ever been anywhere interesting on vacation?

B: Yeah, last year I went to Paris. — Brazil / London / Thailand

A: Really? What was it like?

B: It was amazing! — great / interesting / fun

A: What did you do there?

B: I saw the Eiffel Tower and ate a lot of French food. — visited Rio de Janeiro / learned to surf / saw Buckingham Palace / went to the British Museum / stayed on an island / learned to scuba dive

B. Practice with a partner. Use the words on the right.

C. Practice again. Talk about places you've been.

READING

A. Reading a map. Look at the map. It shows the route of travel writer Andrew Evans' trip.

1. Where did the trip start and end?

   _____

2. How many countries did he travel through?

   a. 7   b. 14   c. 21

🎧 Track 2-04 **B. Scan for numbers.** What do the numbers below refer to? Scan the reading and match. Then read again and check.

10,000 ●	● cents per kilometer in bus fares
1,102.60 ●	● miles traveled
7 ●	● number of buses Evans took
40 ●	● number of days Evans' trip took
42 ●	● total bus fare

U.S.A.

Washington D.C.

MEXICO

HONDURAS

NICARAGUA

GUATEMALA

EL SALVADOR

COSTA RICA

PANAMA

COLOMBIA

ECUADOR

PERU

Pacific Ocean

In Bolivia, Evans traveled through Uyuni, a large area made of salt. He took this photo after it rained. ▼

BOLIVIA

CHILE

ARGENTINA

Ushuaia, Argentina

Drake Passage

Marguerite Bay

ANTARCTICA

Bus to Antarctica

Andrew Evans wanted to go to Antarctica all his life, but he didn't want to go on a tour or spend a lot of money. He wanted a real adventure, so he went by bus. Actually, Evans took 40 buses to travel the 10,000 miles (16,093 km) from his home in Washington, D.C. to the city of Ushuaia at the bottom of South America. It took him 42 days and cost him $1,102.60 total in bus fares—about 7 cents a kilometer. From Ushuaia, he took a ship to Antarctica.

Evans traveled light: he brought a backpack with some clothes, his computer, and cameras. He took video and photos, wrote blog posts, and used Twitter so people around the world could follow his adventure in real time.

What did Evans learn from going by bus? "The bus took longer, yes," he wrote, "but I got to see everything we miss when we travel by plane: The changes from one place to another—and the real size of the Earth."

◄ In Antarctica, Evans posted: "Is this place beautiful? Oh, yes, no land can compare."

C. Sequencing. Andrew Evans sent hundreds of tweets (Twitter messages) on his trip. Put the tweets below in order from first (**1**) to last (**6**).

_____ About 12 miles from entrance to Panama Canal. Can't believe how far I've come in just 2 weeks.

_____ Been on the ship 18 hrs & it feels like I'm back in college: lots of learning, fun homework (take pictures), new friends, work hard/play hard.

_____ Boarded the first bus: Washington, D.C., metrobus S2 to metro center $1.35 ticket! I'm off!

_____ Just finished an incredible Bolivian lunch in a café of El Prado in La Paz. Now repacking for tonight's bus to the south of the country.

_____ Just set foot on Antarctica. My 7th continent & the end of my bus journey!

_____ Safely in Mexico at the Reynosa Bus Station: Bienvenido in Mexico!

LISTENING

Track 2-05
A. Listen for the main idea. Andrew Evans talks about his journey. Is he talking about the beginning or end of his journey?

Track 2-05
B. Listen for details. Circle the words you hear.

"So I made it to Ushuaia. And there was the National Geographic Explorer—the (**ship** / **bus**) that I was going to take.

Two days later, we reached Antarctica. The weather was (**beautiful** / **horrible**). It was snowing and I was (**sad** / **smiling**) because that's exactly how I wanted Antarctica to be—and I finally set foot on the Antarctic continent. I stood on this rock . . . and for a split second, I felt that (**joy** / **happiness**) of really doing something (**difficult** / **different**) and traveling in a way that was different, and achieving a far end of the world that not that many people get to go to."

DISCUSSION

Talking about your dream holiday. Where would you like to go? What would you like to do? Tell a partner. Use the language below.

> I'd really like to go to Egypt. I'd love to see the pyramids.

> Me too! Also, I really want to go to China to see the Great Wall.

The Snowman Trek

The Tiger's Nest Monastery, one place on the Snowman Trek

BEFORE YOU WATCH

About the video. Bhutan is a country high in the Himalaya Mountains. Very few tourists visit the country, and even fewer take the famous "Snowman Trek," a very difficult and long hike. Kira Salak is an American travel writer who completed this trek.

Prediction. Look at the photos. Match the numbers below with what they refer to.

1	days to complete the trek
24	height in meters of the highest point of the climb
340	length of the trek in kilometers
5,300	number of places on the hike that have Internet access
500,000	number of steps the hike takes

WHILE YOU WATCH

Check your answers above.

AFTER YOU WATCH

A. What do you remember? Are the statements below true or false?

	True	False
1. More people have reached the top of Mount Everest than have finished the Snowman Trek.	_____	_____
2. Kira Salak traveled with five teammates.	_____	_____
3. Trekkers use horses and yaks on the trek.	_____	_____
4. Trekkers must climb 6,000 meters high in several places.	_____	_____
5. The highest pass on the climb is the most difficult.	_____	_____
6. Not all the team make it to the end of the trek.	_____	_____

B. Think about your own challenges. In the video, you saw that the Snowman Trek is very long and difficult. Think of a time when you pushed yourself to do something that was difficult or challenging. Complete the table below.

What did you do?	Why was it difficult?	What did you learn?

C. Talk with a partner. Tell a partner about your challenge.

A guide at the highest point on the Snowman Trek

PLAN AN EXPEDITION

You are going to plan an expedition for a group of students.

A. Work with a partner. Read the information about National Geographic Student Expeditions.

National Geographic Student Expeditions is a travel program for students. What can you do?

- Meet local people and learn about their culture and history.
- Learn about photography, filmmaking, or issues like climate change.
- Plant trees, teach local children, or build housing.
- Meet a National Geographic expert (like a biologist or filmmaker), who will join the trip.

B. Create your own expedition. Complete the table.

Where is your expedition to?	What will your students do there?	What will they learn?	Which famous person will come?

C. Present your expedition to another pair. Tell them the name of your expedition and explain it to them. Answer any questions they have.

D. Repeat with other pairs. At the end, choose the expedition you like the most.

Do an online search for "National Geographic Student Expeditions." On the site, click on "Find a Trip." Look at the list of trips and choose one from there.

A group of young people on an expedition to the Galapagos Islands watching a sea lion

THINK ABOUT THE PHOTO

A. Look at the photo. Turn over the page and decide on the best title for the photo:

Maasai Warriors Practice Fighting

Maasai Warriors Show their Traditional Clothing

A Traditional Maasai Dance

Learning to Hunt in Kenya

B. Examine the photo. Look at the photo again. Check (✔) all of the things below that you can find. Add a few words of your own to the list.

☐ Maasai warrior	☐ traditional clothing	☐ horn	☐ sticks
☐ jumping	☐ sandals	_____	_____

DISCUSSION

A. Describe the photo. Work with a partner. Take turns describing the photo to each other.

I see two men jumping.

One man is holding a horn.

B. Talk with a partner. This photo shows Maasai warriors doing a traditional dance. Discuss with your partner:

1. Why do you think Maasai warriors dance?

2. Would you like to learn this dance?

C. Learn more online. Find out more about Maasai warriors on the Internet. Search an online video site for videos of the Maasai dance.

CAPTION COMPETITION

What do you think this man is saying to his friend?

Maasai warriors

Review 3

A. Vocabulary review. Complete each sentence using the words in the box.

| benefit | lyrics | prevent | social issue | talent |

1. My brother has a real _____ for playing the drums.

2. Bullying is a very serious _____.

3. I want to sing this song, but I can't remember the _____.

4. The noise from outside will _____ me from sleeping.

5. I can _____ a lot from learning English.

B. Complete the sentences. Draw lines to match the two halves.

1. Couch surfing is a great way to travel   a. because I post my location on Twitter.

2. I went to Paris   b. because I wanted to see the Eiffel Tower.

3. My friends know where I am   c. because it is difficult.

4. I won't stay at this hotel again   d. because it is inexpensive.

5. Very few tourists complete the trek   e. because it is too noisy.

C. Complete each sentence with your own idea. Then share your ideas with a partner. Does he or she agree with you?

1. _____ is fun.

2. _____ is not safe.

3. _____ is horrible.

4. _____ is challenging.

5. _____ is impossible.

> I think skiing is so much fun. I love it.

> Really? I've never tried it. But I really think surfing is fun.

D. Complete the survey. Complete the questions below with your own ideas. Then interview a partner.

1. What kind of _____ do you like?

2. Who's your favorite _____?

3. Have you ever _____?

4. Which _____ would you like to _____?

7

Family

The grandmother of Jeremy Lin, an American basketball player, showing a family photograph

WARM UP

Answer these questions with a partner.

1. Do you come from a big family?
2. Who in your family are you most like?
3. Is anyone in your family famous?

71

Jacques Cousteau testing new SCUBA equipment

Alexandra Cousteau

A Famous *Family*

LISTENING

Track 2-06

A. Listen for details. Listen to the information about Jacques Cousteau. Circle the correct answers.

Jacques Cousteau is famous for studying the world's oceans. He is also the inventor of (**the submarine** / **SCUBA equipment**) and special (**cameras** / **boats**). In the 1960s and 1970s, Jacques had a popular (**radio** / **TV**) show with his (**son** / **daughter**).

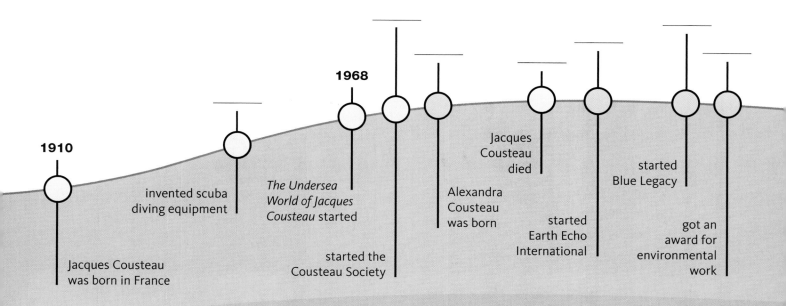

1910 Jacques Cousteau was born in France

invented scuba diving equipment

1968 The Undersea World of Jacques Cousteau started

started the Cousteau Society

Alexandra Cousteau was born

Jacques Cousteau died

started Earth Echo International

started Blue Legacy

got an award for environmental work

 B. Listen for dates. Listen again and write the years for Jacques Cousteau above the blue circles. ◯

 C. Listen and complete the timeline. Listen and write the years for Alexandra Cousteau above the pink circles. ◯

D. Discuss with a partner. Do you know any families who have the same jobs?

> My uncle is a police officer, and so is his son, my cousin.

> Really? My mother and my grandfather are both doctors.

CONVERSATION

A. Listen to the conversation.

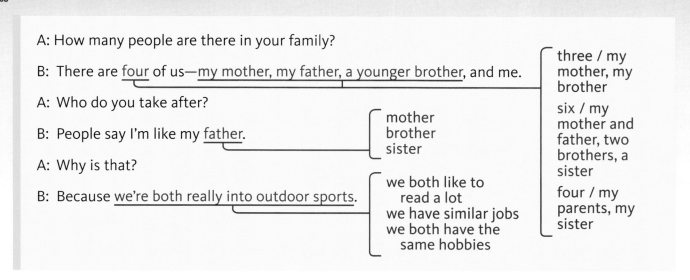

A: How many people are there in your family?

B: There are four of us—my mother, my father, a younger brother, and me.

A: Who do you take after?

B: People say I'm like my father.

A: Why is that?

B: Because we're both really into outdoor sports.

three / my mother, my brother

six / my mother and father, two brothers, a sister

four / my parents, my sister

mother
brother
sister

we both like to read a lot
we have similar jobs
we both have the same hobbies

B. Practice with a partner. Use the words on the right.

C. Practice again. Talk about your own family.

READING

A. Prediction. Look at the pictures below and read the caption. Brazilian families are changing. Are they getting bigger or smaller?

Track 2-09, 2-10

B. Split reading. Student A: Read the passage below. Complete questions 1 and 2 in the table. **Student B: Turn to page 120.**

	Brazilian families in the past	Brazilian families today
1. Family size		
2. Where people live		
3. When people get married		
4. People who own a television		

BRAZIL'S CHANGING FAMILIES

Brazil

In 1960, Brazilian mothers had more than six children on average. By 2009, they had only one or two.

In the past, Brazilian family sizes were much larger than today. In the 1990s, family size suddenly decreased. What is causing these changes?

For years, many Brazilian families had four or more children. However, today, most Brazilian families have only one or two children.

Thirty years ago, many Brazilians lived in small towns. Today, almost 85% of Brazil's people live in cities. Life in a city can be expensive, so a small family is better.

C. Work with a partner. Ask your partner questions to complete the rest of the table.
Student A: Complete questions 3 and 4 of the table on Page 74.
Student B: Turn to page 120.

D. Discuss with a partner. In your opinion, are the changes to Brazilian families mostly good or bad? Why? Tell your partner.

> I think smaller families are better. You can spend more time with each person in your family.

> That's true, but I think that wanting exciting lives like people on TV isn't a good thing.

LISTENING

Track 2-11

A. Listen and complete. Which countries have the highest percentage of people living alone? Look at Chart 1. Can you guess the answers to **a** and **b**? Listen and check.

Percentage of people living alone

Sweden	a. _____
United Kingdom	34%
b. _____	31%

Track 2-12

B. Listen and complete. How old are people who live alone in the U.S.? Write **a**, **b**, and **c** on Chart 2.

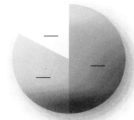

People who live alone in the U.S.A.

a. People aged from 18 to 34

b. People in their 30s, 40s, and 50s

c. People 65 and older

C. What do you think? In your country, are families different than when your parents were young? For each topic, write one sentence about how things have changed. Add your own idea.

	How have things changed?
Age of marriage	
Family size	
Working mothers	
People living alone	
My idea:	

DISCUSSION

Showing you are interested. Work with a partner. **Student A:** Talk about the answers you wrote in the table above. **Student B:** Listen to your partner, and show you are interested. Use the language below.

> Twenty-five years ago, most people got married at 25 or 26. Today, people stay single longer.

> Really? That's really interesting.

> Uh-huh. I see.

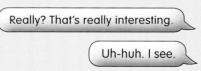

Raising Otter Babies

Missouri, U.S.A.

A group of otters swimming in the water in North Carolina, U.S.A.

BEFORE YOU WATCH

About the video. Biologist Glenn Chambers and his wife Jeannie live in Missouri, in the United States. In the video, they raise two baby otters. The Chambers care for the otter babies just like children. Sometimes they do something bad, like make a mess, but Glenn and Jeannie love them very much.

What do you think? How do you feel about raising wild animals like otters at home? Check (✓) the sentence that you most agree with.

☐ Otters look like fun animals. I'd love to raise them!

☐ Otters in my house? No way! They need a lot of care, and they make a mess.

☐ I think otters and other wild animals need to be in the wild—not in a zoo, and not in a house.

☐ *Your idea:* _____

WHILE YOU WATCH

Watch for details. How do the Chambers care for the otter pups? Check (✓) what you see in the video.

- ☐ They feed them.
- ☐ They watch TV with them.
- ☐ They teach them to swim.
- ☐ They take them to visit schools.
- ☐ They let them play.
- ☐ They sleep beside them at night.
- ☐ They give them baths.
- ☐ They teach them to catch fish.

AFTER YOU WATCH

A. What do you remember? Answer these questions.

1. What do the baby otters eat?
2. What did the otters do in the bathroom?
3. What important job do the otters and the Chambers have to do?
4. Why do the Chambers have to give the otters to the zoo?
5. How did the Chambers feel when they left the otters at the zoo?

B. What do you think? What are some good points about having animals in the house? What are some bad points?

Good points	Bad points

C. Talk with a partner. Share your answers with your partner. Then look back at your answer to the **Before You Watch** question. After watching the video, do you feel the same? Tell your partner.

A family of otters in the wild

Family Debate

In groups of four, you are going to have a debate.

A. Work in a group of four. Read the two statements below and decide which one your group will debate.

1. Big families are better than small families.
2. A mother should stay home with her children and not work.

B. Research your script. Divide your group of four into two pairs. One pair will argue for the statement, and the other will argue against it. Each pair should think of two reasons *for* it **or** two reasons *against* it. You have to explain your reasons, so make some notes.

C. Have a debate. One student from the *for* team will argue for the statement. Then one student from the *against* team will argue against that statement. Then the second student from each team will speak.

D. Choose a winner. Together, decide which team won the debate. For each team decide if the speaker . . .

1. gave two reasons and explained them clearly.
2. used facts and examples.
3. argued well against the other side.

Go online and research your topic. Find facts to support your opinion. Use these in your debate.

In China, one child families, like this one, are very common.

8

Nature

A hiker crossing a river in Greenland

WARM UP

Answer these questions with a partner.

1. Do you like spending time in nature?
2. Where is a good place near you to see nature?
3. What outdoor activities do you enjoy?

LISTENING

Track 2-13

A. Predicting. Match the photographs on page 81 with the descriptions below. Write **A–D**. Then listen and check.

_____ is best known for its beautiful mountain scenery.

_____ is the coldest place on Earth.

_____ is home to millions of wild animals.

_____ is called "the world's largest outdoor museum."

B. Matching. Which activities do you think you can do in each place? Check (✓) them.

	horseback riding	hiking	hot air ballooning	mountain biking	skiing	camping	animal watching
Antarctica							
Luxor							
French Alps							
Serengeti							

Track 2-14

C. Listen. Check your ideas in **B**.

D. Discuss with a partner. Which adventure would you most like to try? Why?

> I want to go skiing in the Alps. I love to ski.

> Mountain biking sounds fun, too.

CONVERSATION

Track 2-15

A. Listen to the conversation.

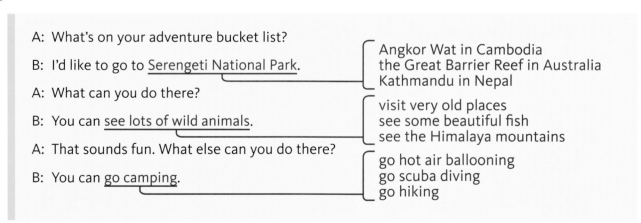

A: What's on your adventure bucket list?

B: I'd like to go to Serengeti National Park.

A: What can you do there?

B: You can see lots of wild animals.

A: That sounds fun. What else can you do there?

B: You can go camping.

Angkor Wat in Cambodia
the Great Barrier Reef in Australia
Kathmandu in Nepal

visit very old places
see some beautiful fish
see the Himalaya mountains

go hot air ballooning
go scuba diving
go hiking

B. Practice with a partner. Use the words on the right.

C. Practice again. Talk about your own bucket list.

My Adventure Bucket List

France —
Egypt —
Tanzania —
Antarctica

A The Valley of the Kings
(Luxor, Egypt)

B The French Alps
(France)

C Antarctica

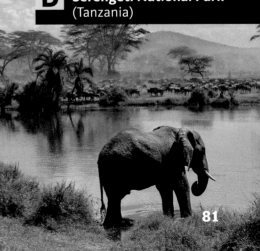

D Serengeti National Park
(Tanzania)

READING

A. Predicting. Look quickly at the passage and photos on the opposite page. Who is Juan Martinez?

    a. a school teacher   b. a farmer   c. a nature tour guide

B. Reading. Read the passage on the next page and check your answer in **A**.

C. Sequencing. Put these events from Juan Martinez's life in order from **1** to **7**.

    a. _____ He failed a science class.   e. _____ His grades improved.

    b. _____ He joined a nature program in Wyoming.   f. _____ He almost joined a gang.

    c. _____ He went to college.   g. _____ His teacher made him join the Eco Club.

    d. _____ He joined an organization to show nature to city kids.

D. Discuss with a partner. Would you like to go on one of Martinez's trips? Why?

LISTENING

A. Read and listen. You will hear an interviewer (I) talking with Juan Martinez (M). Read the question and Martinez's answers. Then listen and circle the words he says.

I: To get kids interested in nature, what do you tell them?

M: It's not so much "Hey, we're going out to nature because we have to take care of the trees." We're going out to nature because it helps you be (**healthy** / **happy**). It helps you live a better (**experience** / **life**). It's gonna improve, you know, your (**math** / **sport**) and (**English** / **science**) skills.

I: These days, why do kids spend less time outdoors?

M: [In the past] nature was such an integral part of everything that happened in everyday life. You know, go out and enjoy the outdoors until the lights come on . . . the street lights come on. That doesn't happen anymore, you know. More and more, we're connected to the (**technology** / **Internet**). And more and more we're connected to (**books** / **ourselves**) but we're not connecting with (**our family** / **each other**) and with nature.

B. Listen again. Check your answers.

DISCUSSION

Talking about pros and cons. Do you think kids who live in the country are happier than kids who live in the city? What are the good and bad things about each place? Tell a partner. Use the language below.

> I think living in the country is better. You can be healthier and get more exercise.

> I don't think so. It isn't as good as living in the city. There aren't as many things to do, and there isn't as much entertainment.

Back to *Nature*

Wyoming

California

Growing up in Los Angeles, California, Juan Martinez's family taught him the importance of education. However, in his neighborhood, there were many gang members. Martinez almost joined a gang, but then something happened. He failed a science class in high school. To pass the class, his teacher said, he had to join the Eco Club and work in the school garden. Later, he had a chance to do a two-week nature program in Wyoming.

Juan Martinez (environmentalist)

"I still can't find the words to describe the first moment I saw those mountains," Martinez says. He saw animals. He went hiking in the Teton Mountains. He slept under the night sky, full of stars. The trip changed him forever. Martinez returned to Los Angeles and his grades improved. He finished school and in time, he went to college. Today, he works for an organization that connects city kids with nature.

The Grand Teton Mountains
(Wyoming, U.S.A.)

Glacier National Park

Salt Lake City

Chihuahua Desert

American Frontier
Journey

Glacier National Park, U.S.A.

BEFORE YOU WATCH

About the video. The video follows two groups of travelers as they travel across the United States. Their whole journey was made through public land.

Vocabulary matching. You will hear the numbers below in the video. Match each number with what it refers to.

2	the number of animal species in Glacier National Park
60	the number of teams on the journey
300	the number of days the journey took
1,000,000	the size of public lands in the United States in square kilometers

WHILE YOU WATCH

A. Check your answers. As you watch, check your answers to the questions above.

B. Watch for details. Write five forms of transportation the team used.

_____ _____ _____

_____ _____

AFTER YOU WATCH

A. What do you remember? Are the statements below true or false?

	True	False
1. The teams only traveled on land controlled by the U.S. government.	_____	_____
2. The team members were volunteers.	_____	_____
3. Team South started their trip from Mexico.	_____	_____
4. The Chihuahua Desert has a large variety of plants and animals.	_____	_____
5. During the trip, the teams stopped to teach people.	_____	_____
6. The two teams finished in different places.	_____	_____

B. Plan a trip. Imagine you are taking a long journey. Where would you go? What would you take with you?

I would go to . . .
I would take . . .

C. Talk with a partner. Tell a partner about your answers above.

Casa Grande Peak, Big Bend
National Park, in the Chihuahua
Desert, U.S.A.

Make a
Public Service
Announcement

A public service announcement (PSA) is a TV, radio, or Internet advertisement with a message. You will make a public service announcement that makes people want to spend more time outdoors.

A. Research your script. Make a list of ideas for a 60-second radio or video PSA.

1. Tell people: *We all need to spend more time outdoors*.
2. Explain why spending time outdoors is good for you.
3. Suggest ideas for places to go and outdoor activities to do there.

B. Write your script. It should be about 60 seconds long.

C. Practice your PSA or create a video for it.

D. Present your PSA to other groups. Listen to theirs. Which PSA was the best? Why? Tell the class.

 Research facts and numbers to use in your PSA. Find photos online or take pictures or video of outdoor places.

Hikers enjoying the scenery from the top of a mountain in Thailand

THINK ABOUT THE PHOTO

A. Examine the photo. Look at the photo on the next page. Check (✓) all of the things below that you can find. Add a few words of your own to the list.

☐ mountains   ☐ climbers   ☐ parachute   ☐ the edge   ☐ valley

☐ trees   ☐ rope   _____   _____   _____

B. Learn about the photo. Complete the description of the photo by choosing the correct words.

Jumping off the 1. (**center / edge**) of Half Dome in Yosemite National Park is against the law. However, the sport of BASE jumping is getting 2. (**more and more / less and less**) popular. BASE jumping means to 3. (**parachute off / climb down**) tall things, like buildings, bridges, and mountains, rather than jump out of an airplane. This photo shows four climbers doing just that. Climbers say that it is more 4. (**fun / difficult**) to jump than to climb all the way back 5. (**up / down**) the mountain.

DISCUSSION

A. Discuss with a partner. What do you like about the photo?

> I like how high up the climbers are.

B. Talk about other photos. Do an Internet search for other BASE jumping photos. Find a photo you like. Show it to your partner and say why you like it.

C. Think about the photo. Do you like high places? Would you like to jump off the edge of a mountain? Why do people do BASE jumping?

D. Interview your classmates. Where is the highest place you have been? How did you feel at the top?

CAPTION COMPETITION

What do you think this jumper is saying?

Climbers BASE jump from the edge of Half Dome in Yosemite National Park, U.S.A.

Review 4

A. Vocabulary review. Complete the sentences using the words in the box.

award	decrease	half	single	urban

1. The director won a(n) _____ for his new movie.
2. My friend doesn't have a boyfriend. She is _____ .
3. Do you want to share? You can have _____ of my pizza.
4. Around the world, more and more people are leaving the countryside to live in _____ areas.
5. I cannot work on Saturdays this year, so my salary will _____ .

B. True or false. Look back at Unit 8. Are the following statements true or false?

	True	False
1. The Valley of the Kings is the coldest place on Earth.	_____	_____
2. Juan Martinez grew up in California.	_____	_____
3. Juan Martinez thinks kids should spend more time outdoors.	_____	_____
4. The two teams of public lands travelers traveled the entire length of Canada.	_____	_____
5. The teams trekked for about two months.	_____	_____

C. Make a quiz. Now look back at unit 7 and write some statements that are true and some that are false. Show your partner. Ask him or her to say whether they are true or false.

D. Talking about pros and cons. Make a list of:

Two cities	_____	_____
Two natural places to visit	_____	_____
Two restaurants	_____	_____
Two items to buy	_____	_____

What are the good and bad things about each one? Tell your partner.

One good thing about Seoul is that there are a lot of good stores there.

Yes, but sometimes I think it's too crowded.

Happiness

New nuns playing ball at their monastery in Arequipa, Peru

WARM UP

Answer these questions with a partner.

1. What are some things that make you happy?
2. Do you think people in your country are generally happy?
3. Which country do you think has the happiest people?

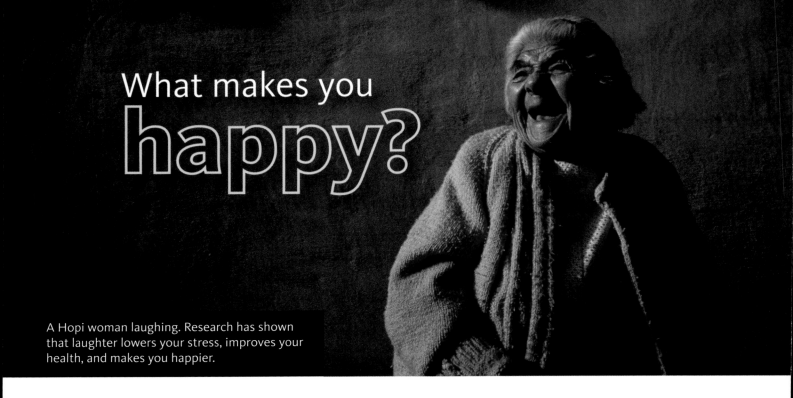

What makes you happy?

A Hopi woman laughing. Research has shown that laughter lowers your stress, improves your health, and makes you happier.

LISTENING

A. What's important for you to be happy? Choose five things from the list below. Rank them from **1** (most important) to **5**.

☐ hobbies   ☐ helping other people   ☐ friends
☐ family   ☐ a good education   ☐ enough money
☐ good health   ☐ a nice house   ☐ a pet
☐ a lot of money   ☐ having goals   ☐ other _____

B. Listen for the main idea. Listen to the beginning of a conversation. Which of these statements are true? Check [✓] all that are correct.

Track 2-18

☐ One person read a book about happiness.
☐ Happiness is different for each person.
☐ Both people like to cook.
☐ Some things make almost everyone happy.

C. Listen for details. Listen and look at the list above in **A**. Which things did the speaker say are important? Circle them.

Track 2-19

D. Discuss with a partner. Show your ranking in **A** to your partner. Say why you chose those things.

> I ranked "a lot of money" number 3. In my opinion, you need money to be happy.

> Really? I don't think you need a lot of money to be happy, but it helps.

CONVERSATION

Track 2-20

A. Listen to the conversation.

A: What do you think people need to be happy?

B: I think <u>money</u> is the most important thing.

good health
a good education
having friends

A: Really? Why do you think that?

B: Because if you have <u>money</u>, you can <u>buy things you want</u>.

good health / do anything you like
a good education / get a better job
friends / have fun with them

A: That's true. I think that's important, but I think <u>your family</u> is important, too.

having children
having enough money
a pet

B. Practice with a partner. Use the words on the right.

C. Practice again. Talk about things that make you happy.

Football fans celebrating
a winning goal

The Happiest Places on EARTH

READING

A. Read. Read the passage on the next page. As you read, try to complete words **1** to **9**.

Track **2-21**
B. Listen for details. Check your answers.

C. Work with a partner. Look again at the list of things that make people happy on page 92. Which ones are common in San Luis Obispo?

D. Talk with a partner. How do you feel about San Luis Obispo? Would you like to live there? Why or why not? Tell a partner.

LISTENING

Track **2-22**
A. Listen for details. Denmark is one of the happiest countries in the world. Listen. Are the sentences below true or false?

Most Danish people	True	False
1. pay high taxes	_____	_____
2. enjoy the long winters	_____	_____
3. spend a lot on healthcare	_____	_____
4. work part time	_____	_____

Cyclists riding to work in Copenhagen, Denmark

Track **2-22**
B. Listen again. Complete the missing information.
1. Danes pay taxes of up to _____ %.
2. _____ % of all Danes are members of a club.
3. _____ % volunteer to help other people.
4. Most Danes work _____ hours each week.
5. They usually have _____ weeks of vacation.
6. Almost _____ % bike to work.

DISCUSSION

Comparing and contrasting two things. With a partner, say how your country is the same as and different than Denmark and San Luis Obispo. Use the language below.

> Both San Luis Obispo and my hometown of Valencia are pretty laid-back.

> People in San Luis Obispo are really healthy, but many people in Valencia smoke.

> Neither Denmark nor my country have low taxes.

San Luis Obispo, U.S.A.

SAN LUIS OBISPO, U.S.A.

A young boy standing in front of a wall of bubblegum in "Bubblegum Alley," San Luis Obispo, U.S.A.

Dan Buettner's book *Thrive* lists it as one of the happiest cities in the U.S. Why?

THE CITY

- is close to both the (1) _o_____ and the mountains. It has a lot of natural beauty and many places to hike or bike.

- is **laid-back**. There are lots of parks, cafés, and open areas where people can relax. Even in the downtown area, there are very few cars and almost no (2) _t_____.

- is very **safe**—many people don't lock their (3) _d_____, day or night.

- has a **lively** arts scene—every summer, there are several free concerts and music and art (4) _f_____.

- is a (5) _h_____ environment. Food is fresh, and there is no (6) _s_____ in restaurants and most outdoor public places.

THE PEOPLE

- are known for their high levels of emotional well-being. They smile more and experience less (7) _s_____ than people in other U.S. cities.

- are very active: many (8) _b_____ to work or school.

- are **sociable**. They spend lot of time with (9) _f_____ and friends. Many also **volunteer** and help others in the community.

95

Hula dancers dance at sunrise in Molokai, Hawaii

An Island Paradise

BEFORE YOU WATCH

About the video. Molokai, in Hawaii, is known as "the Friendly Island." The people who live there are famous for being laid-back and having happy lives.

Read the quotes below. Three of them are from the video, and one of them is not. Which quote is NOT from the video?

1. "Molokai is just a very laid-back, slow pace island. There is no rushing."

2. "Molokai's a very beautiful place, and the people are nice, but sometimes I wish there was a little more excitement."

3. "We don't need whatever the other islands have. We can live with whatever we have here."

4. "A lot of the people that come and visit our island want to make big changes, but you know what? We don't need the changes."

WHILE YOU WATCH

Check your answers. As you watch, check your answer to the question above.

AFTER YOU WATCH

Hawaii, U.S.A.

A. What do you remember? Why are the people in Molokai so happy? Make a list of reasons.

B. What do you think? Do you think Molokai is paradise? Check (✓) the sentence that best describes your opinion.

☐ Yes, this is my idea of paradise. It's beautiful, the people are friendly, and life is laid-back.

☐ I don't understand why people think this is paradise. It's so boring! There's nothing to do.

☐ It looks relaxing. It's nice for a quiet vacation, but I wouldn't want to live there.

C. Talk with a partner. Share your answers to **A**, and explain your answer to **B**.

Molokai from above

97

How to be  HAPPY

In groups of three, you are going to give a timed talk explaining how to be happy.

A. Make a list of ideas. Work in groups of three. Complete the chart with your ideas. Think about things you learned in this unit.

. . . in your community	. . . at school or work	. . . in your social life
1. *Live somewhere safe.*	1. *Make friends with a classmate or co-worker.*	1. *Join a club.*
2. _____	2. _____	2. _____
. . . about money	**. . . at home**	**. . . by yourself**
1. *Try not to borrow money.*	1. *Paint your room a happy color.*	1. *Find a hobby.*
2. _____	2. _____	2. _____

B. Choose ideas to talk about. Each person in the group should choose two areas in the chart to talk about.

C. Prepare and practice your talk. Your group has three minutes to speak. Each person in the group speaks for one minute (30 seconds for each area). Explain how your ideas can improve a person's happiness. **See page 124 for ideas**.

D. Give your talk to another group. The other group will listen and decide how many points your team gets. A group can get a total of 9 points—up to 3 points for each speaker who explains his or her point clearly in one minute.

Use a computer to prepare your presentation. Prepare six slides—one for each area in your chart. On each slide, list your ideas. Time the slides so each one moves forward every 30 seconds during your talk.

A butterfly lands on a young boy at Folsom Children's Zoo, U.S.A.

Conservation

An endangered gorilla hiding
in the forest in Rwanda

WARM UP

Answer these questions with a partner.

1. What endangered species do you know?
2. Why are some species endangered?
3. What can people do to help endangered species?

LISTENING

Track 2-23

A. Listen for the main idea. Look at the pictures on the right. Listen and number the animals in the order you hear about them.

Track 2-23

B. Listen for numbers. Listen again. Complete the table using the numbers in the box.

| 1,000 | 1,600 | 21,000 | 50,000 | 200,000 | 500,000 | 1,200,000 |

	Population in the 1970s	Population today	Which of these has affected them?		
			Poison and pesticides	Habitat loss	Hunting and poaching
Giant Panda	1,000				
African Lions					
African Elephants					
Bald Eagles					

Track 2-24

C. Listen for details. Why is each species endangered? Check (✓) the correct boxes in the table.

D. Discuss with a partner. What else do you know about the endangered species on the next page?

> I saw some giant pandas on a TV show last week. The babies are so small!

CONVERSATION

Track 2-25

A. Listen to the conversation.

A: Did you know that grizzly bears are endangered?

B: Yeah? Why are they endangered?

A: Mainly because of hunting by humans and habitat loss.

B: How many are left?

A: Only about 25,000.

- snow leopards
- Tasmanian devils
- black rhinos

- habitat loss and poaching
- disease
- poaching

- Fewer than 6,000
- Between 10 and 15,000
- Fewer than 5,000

B. Practice with a partner. Use the words on the right.

C. Practice again. Research and talk about other endangered species.

Why are they endangered?

lions

bald eagle

giant panda

elephant

Solving problems, saving animals

READING

A. Predicting. These conservationists are working to save animals. Look at the picture below and the one **on page 126**. Match the people to the problems they are solving and the place where they work.

Vathana   •   • freshwater fish   •   • Cambodia

Zeb Hogan   •   • elephants   •   • Mongolia

Track 2-26, 2-27

B. Split reading. Student A: Read the passage below about Zeb Hogan. **Student B: Turn to page 126** and read about Vathana.

Zeb Hogan

Many of the world's largest freshwater fish are endangered. In Mongolia, for example, people who live near the rivers and lakes are often poor. They kill the fish for food, decreasing their numbers. People also kill them for sport, so their numbers are further decreasing. Zeb Hogan, from the United States, is working with local people to save fish such as the giant salmon in Mongolia. Hogan is part of a project to bring tourists to rivers in Mongolia. They pay to catch salmon for sport, and then release them—throw them back into the water. The fish are not hurt, and the people in Mongolian villages make money from the tourism.

(right) A woman selling a Mekong catfish at a market in Laos. These fish are critically endangered. Zeb Hogan (left) is working to protect giant fish like this.

C. What do you remember? Tell your partner about the conservationist you read about.

D. Who are these sentences about? Student A: Complete the table below asking your partner questions. **Student B: Complete the table on page 126.** Don't look at your partner's reading passage! Check (✓) the correct answers.

This conservationist . . .	Zeb	Vathana
works to protect endangered species.		
works with local people to protect animals.		
brings tourists to the country.		
builds schools.		
uses fireworks and hot pepper.		

LISTENING

Track **2-28**

A. Listen for the main idea. Paula Kahumbu is the director of a website, wildlifedirect.com. What is the site's aim?

a. to let tourists book holidays to see endangered species

b. to let conservationists share information about their work

Track **2-28**

B. Listen for details. Circle the correct answers.

1. Paula Kahumbu is from _____ .

   a. Kenya   b. South Africa   c. Canada

2. Wildlifedirect.com includes information about _____ different conservation projects.

   a. 20   b. 120   c. 220

3. What can people do at wildlifedirect.com to help conservationists with their work?

   a. send money   b. upload photographs
   c. help do scientific research

4. Which of these conservation projects does the listening passage NOT mention?

   a. orangutans in Indonesia   b. gorillas in the Congo
   c. polar bears in Alaska

Paula Kahumbu

DISCUSSION

Talking about problems and solutions. Work with a partner. Discuss a conservation problem you know about, and talk about ways you can help. Use the language below.

> What can we do to help rhinos in Africa?

> We can raise money to send to conservation groups.

> Yeah. Or we could make a poster to tell people about the problem.

Saving
Orphan Elephants

A keeper and an orphan elephant
at the elephant nursery

Kenya

BEFORE YOU WATCH

About the video. At the David Sheldrick Wildlife Trust's Nairobi Elephant Nursery in Kenya, humans raise orphan elephants (elephants with no mothers) until they can return to the wild.

A. Study the graph. Look at the graph. Which statement describes Kenya's elephant population?

a. The population decreased between 1973 and 1989, but is now slowly going up.

b. The population has been decreasing since 1973.

c. The population rose between 1973 and 1989, but is now falling again.

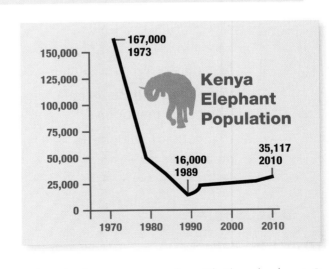

167,000
1973

Kenya
Elephant
Population

35,117
2010

16,000
1989

B. Prediction. What things do you think the keepers at the elephant nursery do with the elephants?

☐ feed them
☐ play with them
☐ ride on their backs
☐ show them to tourists
☐ sleep next to them
☐ teach them to do tricks

WHILE YOU WATCH

Check your answers. As you watch, check your answers to **Before You Watch B**.

AFTER YOU WATCH

A. What do you remember? Are the statements below true or false?

	True	False
1. The orphanage has saved more than 100 elephants.	_____	_____
2. Keepers feed the baby elephants cows' milk.	_____	_____
3. Baby elephants like to be alone.	_____	_____
4. Baby elephants behave like human babies.	_____	_____
5. Orphan elephants are often released back into the wild.	_____	_____
6. In the last 30 years, about 2.5 million elephants have died.	_____	_____

B. Think about it. In this unit you learned about four conservationists and conservation groups— Zeb Hogan, Vathana, Paula Kahumbu, and the Elephant Nursery. Whose conservation work would you most like to volunteer to help? Explain your answer.

C. Talk with a partner. Share your answers to **B** with your partner.

Keepers with a group of baby elephants

Give a *persuasive* presentation

Your class must decide on one endangered species to volunteer to help. In pairs, you will give a presentation to persuade the class to join you.

A. Choose a species. Work with a partner. You are going to give a presentation about an endangered animal. Decide which animal you would like to talk about.

B. Research the animal. Find answers to the questions below.

Where does it live?	
Why is it in danger?	
How many are left?	
Who is working to save it?	
What are they doing?	

C. Prepare your presentation. Think of reasons why people should help the species you have chosen.

D. Give your presentation. Tell the class about your animal and why it should be saved.

E. Decide on the animal to save. As a class, decide which pair's presentation was most persuasive.

Use the Internet to find other people who are trying to help your animal. Find out what you can do to help them.

The San Lucas marsupial frog, from Ecuador, is endangered because of habitat loss.

THINK ABOUT THE PHOTO

A. Complete the description. Complete the information about the photo on the next page.

costumes	cub	feed	first	human	keepers	wild

A person dressed as a panda is holding giant panda _____, Tao Tao, in a training camp at the Wolong Nature Reserve, China. In July 2010, the Nature Reserve started to train giant pandas to be returned into the _____. Tao Tao is the _____ animal in the program. The _____ at the center wear panda _____ when they need to check the baby pandas or _____ them. This is to reduce _____ influence in the pandas' environment.

B. Think of a title for this photo. Then share your title with the class and vote on the best one.

_____

DISCUSSION

A. Describe the photo. Work with a partner. Take turns describing the photo to each other.

> There is a person wearing a panda costume.

> Yes, that person is a keeper at the center.

B. Discuss with a partner. Do you think it is a good idea for the people to wear panda costumes? Why or why not?

CAPTION COMPETITION

What do you think the person holding the cub is thinking? Tell a partner.

Keepers and a panda at Wolong
Nature Reserve, China

Review 5

A. Complete each sentence with vocabulary from unit 9.

1. This weekend, I'm going to _____ to clean up my neighborhood.

2. Next year, the government is going to increase _____ and we will all have to pay more money.

3. Please don't stand near the edge—it's not _____.

4. My brother never comes out of his room. He isn't very _____.

5. This park is always so full of people. It's a very _____ place.

B. Unscramble the letters to make words from unit 10. Match the words to their definitions.

| coreptt | sharfreetw | smarf | socpr | xtintec |

1. A species of animal that no longer exists is _____.

2. _____ are areas of land used for growing food.

3. Plants that are grown for food are _____.

4. If you keep someone safe, you _____ him or her.

5. Some fish live in the sea; others live in lakes or rivers. These are _____ fish.

C. What makes you happy? Write down five things that make you happy. For example, *Having a big house makes me happy.* Then gesture or draw your sentences and have your partner guess the things that make you happy.

D. Work with a partner. Make a list of problems and discuss with your partner how to solve these problems.

> There are many endangered animals in the world.

> Governments might give money to help protect endangered animals.

> The roads in this city are too dangerous for cyclists.

> The city should build more bicycle paths.

EXPANSION ACTIVITY: Talking about Restaurants

Kinds of food

fast food, international food, slow food (local or traditional food), healthy snacks, tasty desserts

Location (Where is it?)

in a nice neighborhood, in a hotel, near the beach, in a food court, at a night market, in a park, near a bus or train station, in a theater or club

Why is it special?

It serves seafood from Hokkaido.; It has live music.; Its ice cream is made fresh every day.; The waiters are robots.; Everything costs $2 or less.

TARGET VOCABULARY

Lesson A

crunchy	Food that is **crunchy** is nicely hard and makes a noise when you eat it.
refreshing	A **refreshing** drink makes you feel cool when you are hot, or energetic when you are tired.
salty	Something that is **salty** tastes like salt.
spicy	**Spicy** food is strongly flavored with spices, for example, a curry.
sweet	**Sweet** food and drink contains a lot of sugar.

Lesson B

affect	If something **affects** another thing, it makes it change in some way.
consume	If you **consume** something, you eat or drink it.
diet	Your **diet** is the kind of food you usually eat.
healthy	Something that is **healthy** is good for your body.
memory	Your **memory** is your ability to remember things.

Other useful words from the unit

alcohol	snack	fast/instant/natural food	organic
tax	vegetarian	vending machine	

IMPORTANT LANGUAGE

Saying you like or don't like a food	
:)	:(
It's delicious / It's tasty / It's yummy.	It's awful / It's disgusting / It's gross.

Saying you agree or disagree	
I think pizza is the best snack.	I agree. I love it. I disagree. In my opinion, salad is much tastier.

PROJECT

Using presentation software, create a presentation about the restaurant you talked about in the Expansion Activity. Include photos of some of the foods you want to serve. Talk about your prices. Show on a map where your restaurant will be.

DISCUSSION

Make and respond to suggestions. You and a partner are going to the Festival in the Desert. Make suggestions for what to do, and listen to your partner's suggestions. **Student B:** Use the language below.

> How about finding a local guide to take us there?

> Yeah, that's a good idea.

> No, let's join another group of tourists and go with them instead.

EXPANSION ACTIVITY: Talking about Festivals

Kinds of festivals

a back-to-school festival, an art and music festival, a food festival, a shopping festival, a science fair, a career fair (to help students get jobs), a sports festival, a holiday festival (e.g., to celebrate Halloween, spring, etc.), a student film festival

Reasons for festivals

to welcome new students, to learn about foods of the world, to celebrate the start of spring

Festival activities

parades, contests, fireworks, games, a dance, music, guest speakers, items for sale

TARGET VOCABULARY

Lesson A

A **contest** is a competition or game.

An **event** is something that happens, especially something that is planned and organized.

Fireworks are things that burn brightly in a beautiful way and make noise. They are used at festivals or at special events.

A **parade** is a line of people or vehicles that moves slowly through an area to celebrate a special event.

Lesson B

If you **celebrate** something, you do something fun because of a special occasion.

A **local** person lives in the area you are talking about.

A **guide** is someone who shows tourists around a place.

In a **performance**, a musician or actor sings, dances, or acts in front of other people.

IMPORTANT LANGUAGE

Making and responding to suggestions		
Making suggestions		**Responding to suggestions**
Let's . . .	ride our bikes to the festival.	***Saying yes***
Why don't we . . .	ride our bikes to the festival?	Great idea! Let's do it.
How about . . .	riding our bikes to the festival?	I like that idea.
What about . . .		(That) sounds good.
		Saying no and suggesting another idea
		(Sorry) but I don't have a bike.
		How about taking the bus instead?
		Or we could take the bus.

PROJECT

Make an online ad for the festival you talked about in the Expansion Activity. Use photos, music, and/or video in your presentation. Put the ad on an online video hosting site or show it to your class.

TARGET VOCABULARY

Lesson A

If something is **ancient**, it is very old.

A **crowded** place is full of people.

A **lively** place has a lot of exciting or interesting things happening there.

Something that is **modern** is new and has the latest ideas.

If something is **popular**, it is liked by a lot of people.

Something that is **trendy** is very fashionable and modern.

Lesson B

If you **commute**, you travel a long distance to work every day.

Noise is a loud or unpleasant sound.

Pollution is poison in the environment that makes it dirty or dangerous to live in.

Public transportation, such as buses or trains, takes people from one place to another.

If you **reduce** something, you make it smaller.

Traffic refers to all the vehicles moving along the road in a particular area.

IMPORTANT LANGUAGE

Giving directions	
Use these **verbs** to explain how to go somewhere.	**Walk up/down** the street. **Cross** the street/bridge. **Turn** left/right. **Go** straight.

Use these **prepositions** to say where a place is.	It's . . .
	    in Taksim Square / Retiro Park / downtown Seoul.
	    on Elgin Street / Nanjing Road / the corner.
	    near subway stop 2.
	    next to a bike shop.
	    across from the train station.

Talking about problems	
There are too many noisy dogs. **There's too much** crime.	**There aren't enough** cinemas. **There isn't enough** excitement.

PROJECT

Take the Urban 100 Challenge! Take 100 photographs over a 500-meter walk. Then share your pictures with your class and your friends. Or put all your pictures together into a film, like *Urban Earth*.

What did you see? What did your friends see? Did anything surprise you?

READING

Track **1-22**

B. **Split reading. Student B:** Read the passage below about bioengineers.

FUTURE OCCUPATIONS
Bioengineer

What occupations will be popular in the future? A recent study lists over 100 possibilities. Here's one: bioengineer.

A man loses an arm in a car accident. A soccer player has a bad knee. In the future, bioengineers will make new body parts for these people, using the person's own cells. Today, scientists are already making some parts, such as ears and skin. In the future, they will make many others.

In the future, bioengineers will not only help sick or injured people. They will also help the elderly. People will live longer, and as they age they will need new body parts. Some say that in the future, another group—professional athletes— will use bioengineers the most. Teams will hire bioengineers to make injured players better and the healthy ones stronger and faster. It will be a new type of sports medicine, and possibly the beginning of super athletes.

An artificial heart. In the future, bioengineers may be able to grow new hearts and other body parts from a person's own cells.

READING

C. **Work with a partner.** Which job(s) are these statements about? **Student B:** Ask your partner questions to help you complete the table below.

	space tour guide	bioengineer
1. This job will allow you to help athletes.	___	___
2. This job will take you away from home for a long time.	___	___
3. This job will help people live healthily for longer.	___	___
4. This job will be more popular in the future.	___	___
5. To do this job, you need to know about science.	___	___

TARGET VOCABULARY

Lesson A

If you do something **solo**, you do it alone.

If something is **rewarding**, it makes you feel happy and satisfied.

If you are **good with kids**, children feel comfortable with you.

If you are **creative**, you have a good imagination, and think of original ideas.

Job titles: cleaner, explorer, teacher, actor, scientist, journalist, dentist, artist, pilot, entrepreneur, shop assistant, coach

Lesson B

Your **occupation** is your job.

If something is **in demand**, it is popular.

Experience is the knowledge you get in a job or activity because you do it for a long time.

Skill is the ability to do something well.

If you are **injured**, you are hurt.

IMPORTANT LANGUAGE

Making predictions about the future	
In the future, people **will** travel in space. **I'll** probably get a part-time job this summer. Without a degree, you **won't** get the job.	Use **will** + base form of the verb to give general information about the future or to make predictions. In speaking, a pronoun (*I, she, he, we, you*) + **will** is often said as *I'll, he'll, you'll*, etc. **won't** = **will not**
Will he get the job? / Where **will** he work?	Notice how to form yes/no and Wh- questions with **will**.
I bet he**'ll** get the job. He**'ll probably** get the job. **I'm not sure. Maybe** he**'ll** get the job and maybe he won't. *	When you make predictions, you can use the words in bold to say how sure you are about something. *I bet* = I'm almost certain. *Probably* = I think it's mostly true. *I'm not sure. / Maybe.* = It's possible, but I don't know.

* When you're not sure about something, you can also use the word *might*: *He **might** get the job, but I'm not sure.*

PROJECT

Interview someone about their job. Outside class, interview a family member or someone you know about their job. Use the questions in the Expansion Activity to start. Tell your class what you learned.

TARGET VOCABULARY

Lesson A

types of musical instruments: didgeridoo, steel drums, horsehead violin
kinds of music: hip-hop, rap, pop, dance music, classical, jazz, R&B, rock, traditional

Lesson B

A **social issue** is an important problem in society.
The **message** of a book or song is the main idea it wants to say or teach.
A song's **lyrics** are its words.
If you **prevent** something, you stop it before it happens.
A **talent** is a special skill or ability.
If you **have a responsibility** to do something, you should do it because it is the right thing to do.
If something **benefits** someone, it helps them or makes a difference.

IMPORTANT LANGUAGE

Talking about likes and dislikes		
😊	😐	😞
I love . . .	I like some . . .	I don't like . . . / I can't stand . . .
I really like . . .	. . . is okay / all right.	I'm not a big fan of . . .

Giving reasons using *because*	
I have a large number of jazz CDs **because** I really like jazz.	I always carry a cloth shopping bag **because** I don't want to use plastic bags.

PROJECT

Make a music video. Find music to go with the song you wrote in the Expansion Activity. Sing your song with the music and make a music video. Share your music video with your class, or upload it to a video hosting website.

TARGET VOCABULARY

Lesson A

Your **host** is the person whose house you are staying at.

A **social networking** site is a website like Facebook, where people can contact other people on the site and be friends with them.

A **member** of a group is someone who belongs to the group.

If something is **inexpensive**, it doesn't cost much money.

A **tourist** is someone who visits a place for fun on vacation.

Lesson B

A **fare** is the money you pay to travel on a trip, for example, on a bus or airplane.

If you **travel light**, you don't take much luggage with you.

If you **miss** something, you don't see or notice it.

When you **make it** somewhere, you arrive there, usually after a difficult journey.

If you **set foot on** (or **in**) a place, you enter that place.

If something happens for **a split second**, it happens for a very short time.

IMPORTANT LANGUAGE

Talking about traveling	
He **flew** from Rio to Sao Paulo. I **ride my bike** to school every day. Let's **take a taxi** to the train station.	There are many ways to travel from one place to another: • You can **drive** or **fly**. • You can **ride a bike**, **motorcycle**, or **scooter**. • You can **take** a **bus**, **train**, **ship/ferry**, or **taxi**.
By plane, it takes an hour to get to Sao Paulo from Rio. **By train** or **car**, it takes about five hours. Andrew Evans saw a lot more because he went/traveled **by bus**.	To explain how you travel somewhere, you can also use *by* + **type of transportation**. The words *go* or *travel* sometimes come before *by* + **type of transportation**.
It takes an hour to fly from Rio to Sao Paulo. **It took** Andrew 40 days to reach Ushuaia.	To explain how long a trip is, use *It takes* + **time**.

Talking about your dream holiday
I'd really love to go to Mexico. **I want to** visit China. **I'd like** to go hiking in Nepal.

PROJECT

Make a brochure for your trip. Make a brochure to tell people about the trip you planned in the Expansion Activity. Include photographs and maps of the places people on the trip will visit. Plan a schedule, so people who are interested in the trip know what they will do and see each day.

READING

Track 2-10

B. Split reading. Student B: Read the passage below. Complete rows 3 and 4 in the table.

	Brazilian families in the past	Brazilian families today
1. Family size		
2. Where people live		
3. When people get married		
4. People who own a television		

BRAZIL'S CHANGING FAMILIES

Brazil

In 1960, Brazilian mothers had more than six children on average. By 2009, they had only one or two.

In the past, Brazilian family sizes were much larger than today. In the 1990s, family size suddenly decreased. What is causing these changes?

In the past, people started families in their early twenties. Today, many young men and women are going to school and getting a job first. They get married and have families later.

In 1980, only about half of all homes had a television. Today, most homes have a TV, and evening shows called *novelas* are very popular. The men and women on these shows are single or have small families. They have exciting lives. People watching want this life, too.

C. Work with a partner. Ask your partner questions to complete the rest of the table.

TARGET VOCABULARY

Lesson A

When you **invent** something, you are the first person to think of it or make it.

If you **take after** a member of your family, you look or behave like them.

If you **win an award**, you get a prize for doing something good.

Lesson B

If women in a particular country have six children **on average**, it means that that is the normal number for women in that area.

If a number **decreases**, it gets smaller.

Half of something is 50% of it.

A **single** person is not married.

Urban means belonging to, or relating to, a city or town.

USEFUL LANGUAGE

Showing you are interested	
My grandfather had 12 brothers and sisters.	Really? That's really interesting. Wow! That's amazing.
In my country, families usually only have one child.	Uh-huh. I see.

PROJECT

Create a poster or presentation. Choose the side of the debate that you personally agree with, and create a poster or use presentation software to present it. Use the Internet for research and find photographs or charts to support your position. Share your poster or presentation with your class.

TARGET VOCABULARY

Lesson A

A **bucket list** is a list of things you would like to do before you die.

The **scenery** in a country area is the land, water, or plants that you can see around you.

Outdoor activities: (go) bungee jumping, (go) camping, (go) hiking, (go) horseback riding, (go) hot-air ballooning, (go) mountain biking, (go) skiing, (go) swimming

Lesson B

If you **join** a group, you become a member of it.

If you **fail** to do something you were trying to do, you do not succeed in doing it.

If you **pass** an exam or test, you get a successful result in it.

When something **improves**, it gets better.

If you **connect** things together, you join them together.

IMPORTANT LANGUAGE

Talking about outdoor activities	
Leo **skis** very well.	In this sentence, *ski* is a verb.
I **like/love/hate/know how/want to ski**.	The infinitive (*to ski*) can follow certain verbs.
Skiing is fun.	In this sentence, *skiing* is a noun (called a gerund).
I **enjoy/like/love/hate/quit skiing**.	The gerund (*skiing*) can follow certain verbs.
Let's **go skiing** this weekend. My brother **goes running** every morning. We **went dancing** last night.	It's common to use *go* + gerund (*go skiing*) to talk about doing outdoor activities that end in *–ing* (*skiing, running, dancing, hiking, swimming*, etc.).

Talking about pros and cons	
Talking about pros	**Talking about cons**
I think living in the country is **better**.	The country **isn't as** interesting as the city.
There are **more** trees and animals.	**There aren't as many** things to do.
You can be **healthier**.	**There isn't as much** entertainment.

PROJECT

Create a video public service announcement. Use words, images, and music to convince people to spend more time in nature. When you are finished, show to your classmates or upload it to a video hosting website.

EXPANSION ACTIVITY: Giving a short presentation

Give a short presentation

Introduce your topic

I am going to talk today about how to be happy in your community and at school.

State the first main idea. Then explain it.

Let's talk first about community.

To be happy in your community, you should . . . because . . . .

You should also . . . because . . .

Doing these things will make you happy in your community.

State the second main idea. Then explain it.

Let's talk next about school.

To be happy at school, you should . . . because . . . .

You should also . . . because . . . .

Doing these things will make you happy at school.

TARGET VOCABULARY

Lesson A

If you feel **stress**, you are worried about difficulties in your life.

A person in **good health** is fit and well.

Education involves teaching and learning.

Your **goals** are things that you want to do.

Lesson B

A **laid-back** person behaves in a relaxed way and doesn't worry about things.

Sociable people are friendly and enjoy talking to other people.

A **volunteer** is someone who does work without being paid for it.

Healthcare services prevent and treat sickness.

Downtown places are in or around the center of a large town or city.

Your **emotional well-being** is your happiness.

IMPORTANT LANGUAGE

Comparing and contrasting two things

When you **compare** things, you talk about ways in which they are similar.

*In **both** Mexico and Colombia, people speak Spanish.*

***Neither** Saudi Arabia nor Singapore have cold winters.*

When you **contrast** things, you talk about ways in which they are different.

*Japan has a lot of active volcanoes, **but** Australia has none.*

PROJECT

Make a movie about happiness. With a camera, take photos or video of things that make you happy or people who are happy. Make a movie from your photos or video, and add music or words to your movie. Upload your movie to an online video hosting site or show it to your class.

READING

Track **2-27**

B. Read the passage. Read the passage below about Vathana.

Tuy Sereivathana (Vathana) meeting U.S. president Barack Obama after winning an environmental award for his work to save elephants

Tuy Sereivathana (Vathana)

In Cambodia, there are many new towns, roads, and farms, and elephant habitats are disappearing. Because of this, elephants go into villages and eat the crops. Poor farmers kill them to protect their land. As a result, the Cambodian elephant population has fallen from 2,000 in 1995 to fewer than 500 today.

Tuy Sereivathana (known as Vathana), from Cambodia, is working to save Asian elephants. He builds schools where students learn about conservation. Also, he teaches farmers ways to keep their land safe from elephants, so farmers don't kill them. For example, he shows them how to use fireworks to scare elephants, or to put hot chili peppers on fences around their fields. The farmers keep their crops, and the elephants keep their lives.

C. What do you remember? Tell your partner about the conservationist you read about.

D. Who are these sentences about? Complete the table below, asking your partner questions. Don't look at your partner's reading passage! Check (✓) the correct answers.

This conservationist . . .	Zeb	Vathana
works to protect endangered species.		
works with local people to protect animals.		
brings tourists to the country.		
builds schools.		
uses fireworks and hot pepper.		